The Entrepreneur Within

Dedication

The inspiration for writing this book resulted from the funeral of my friend Adrian Bazar of blessed memory, who passed away a few years ago. During the eulogy I learned things about him that I had never known. Somehow I felt that our friendship would have been much richer had I been aware of the depth of his life.

I am also aware of how little I know of my parents' and grandparents' aspirations. I want to ensure, therefore, that my children, grandchildren, friends and colleagues know something more about me from my own perspective - perhaps as a kind of 'living will'.

This book is dedicated to my daughters Judy, Rachel and Anna and to my grandchildren and their future families, my friends, my relations, the people I work with and have worked with. It explains who I am and how I progressed from a boy leaving school at 14 to become the founder of the Academy for Chief Executives.

The Entrepreneur *Within*

Brian Chernett

The Entrepreneur Within
First published in 2010 by;
Ecademy Press
48 St Vincent Drive, St Albans, Herts, AL1 5SJ
info@ecademy-press.com
www.ecademy-press.com

Printed and Bound by; **Lightning Source** in the UK and USA
Set in Myriad Pro and Franklin Gothic Medium by Karen Gladwell
Cover artwork and illustrations by Michael Inns

Printed on acid-free paper from managed forests. This book is
printed on demand, so no copies will be remaindered or pulped.

ISBN 978-1-905823-74-1

Contents

Acknowledgments

I am grateful to the people who have inspired me to write this book and supported me as I have put together the words, rewritten the words and in the end produced something which may bore or delight. At last I have produced something in writing about my life, aspirations and much of the learning I have felt of value to pass on.

My wife Jaclyn, who has constantly supported the work that I have done, encouraged me in the writing of this book.

Mindy Gibbins-Klein, the Book Midwife who initially found me, heard me and took me on. Without her this book would have never appeared.

Andy Coote of Bizwords. Andy took my raw data, rewrote it and then rewrote it again and has continued to work with it to ensure that it is well written but within my personal individual style.

Janice Aarons, my long-suffering Personal Assistant, who painstakingly worked through typing and retyping the manuscript.

Mike Burnage, who patiently retyped parts of the book and encouraged me to carry on until I had finished.

Michael Inns and Karen Gladwell, who have put their inimitable creative style into the book and its production.

And to all the other people mentioned and not mentioned in the book who have been my mentors, helping me to live a fulfilled life where great conversations happen all the time.

Introduction

"If you want to see change, be the change you want to see in the world."

Mahatma Gandhi

Why I wrote this book

Not so long ago, a quiet voice within me began telling me it was time to share my knowledge and experience with others, to help them in their lives and in their business. Writing a book was not a conscious goal, but rather part of a growing sense of needing to give back.

Early in 2006 at a network meeting, I met a joyful and encouraging lady called Mindy. We were going around the table discussing what we wanted out of this meeting and Mindy said her company, The Book Midwife, was looking for someone, a businessman in particular, to help write a book. She had helped over a hundred people write business books, personal development books and novels. Now she was looking for a really successful business person to bring their book to life and document their success for the next generation of business people. Something inside of me, perhaps my ego, said that this was the moment. So I went up to Mindy and said *'I have no idea what I want to write a book about. I'm not even sure I want to write a book and I don't know what it would be called, but something inside me is saying the time is now right.'*

During a three and a half hour coaching session with Mindy, I came up with the purpose of the book and the reasons why I wanted to write it. Or should I say 'purposes' because the more I started to reflect on what I wanted from this book project, the more reasons I found to do it.

The main purpose of the book is to provide a legacy for my family; my children, grand-children and their children. It will also be a legacy for those people who continue to work within the company that I created. There are many experiences that have been instrumental in my becoming who I am today. I believe that those experiences enable me to help other entrepreneurs become the best they can be. Some of these experiences have been shared in the past, but they have never been brought together and presented as a coherent model.

The secondary purpose was to remove the self-doubt, the belief that I had since I was fourteen and a half when I left school, that I was unable to write a book, that my English was not good enough and that I lacked the basis of a degree or any other academic award. If I could remove perceived limitations, then that would also be a true sense of achievement.

Leading up to that decision, I had been to several funerals where a eulogy was read about the person who had died. A very good friend of mine died recently and, at his funeral, I heard so much about that person, about how he thought, about his dreams and about his achievements. I found out so much that I had not known about him in his lifetime. Had I known about it, our relationshp could have been so much richer, I would have learned so much more from him and understood more about what 'made him tick'.

So this is my legacy. My purpose is to inspire entrepreneurs and business leaders to achieve their dreams and if they don't know what they are, to help them find them. Over the period of my life and, in particular, over the last seventeen years, I have helped entrepreneurs achieve their dreams and goals and enabled them to spend more time working with family and friends to do the same for them.

It was my intuition that told me to speak to Mindy. It was a belief that I could do it and it required that I take action. It required me to move towards something that was outside myself and told me that Mindy was the right person to work with. It inspired me to write this book and, in the process, I have discovered even more – more insights, more stories that lay just under the surface and more empathy with business leaders everywhere.

As is often the case with these things, the process was to prove almost more important than the actual work. It has allowed me to gather and reflect on my own thoughts and beliefs in order to put them down on paper and, in doing so, I am able to share my very best insights with you - my 'wisdom' if you can call it that. If it helps you even half as much as it has helped me, then I will have achieved my purpose.

At a time when entrepreneurs are often depicted in the media as being ruthless and hard, I also want to make the case for becoming a business leader and entrepreneur while remaining caring and compassionately human. I hope that I can make that case in the pages that follow.

What is leadership?

Leaders take their teams, their followers, into new and unknown territory or into familiar territory but with unfamiliar or innovative products or services. There are many types of leaders ranging from those who stride out ahead and expect their team to follow, to those who encourage and cajole their teams to higher performance that takes the team to new places. I'll talk more about leadership styles and approaches within the later chapters.

Leaders are not necessarily the same as managers, though a leader may need to function as a manager and a manager may also be a leader. It is less about the person and more about what it is they are doing. When we are acting as managers, we are usually working within a set of guidelines and aiming for known and definable goals, often within budgets and timetable constraints. When we are operating as leaders, there are no predetermined goals, other than those of improving and developing the business in as effective a way as possible. Leaders operate with a wide field of vision whilst managers are often narrowly focused. Having said that, it is easy to get hung up on these definitions and miss the point that all of us are leaders *(or could be)* in some aspect of our working and private lives. Leaders become entrepreneurs when they back that vision and create something that didn't exist before.

We need entrepreneurs. Whether or not you believe that the leaders and entrepreneurs of the past have delivered us a world that we can approve of, we need entrepreneurs to take us forward to our dream of a future world. You may not achieve all of your dreams, but if you show no leadership at all, you can be sure that you will achieve none of them.

As Mahatma Gandhi once said, if you want to see change, be the change you want to see in the world. Or to borrow a slogan from more recent times - 'just do it!'

Leading with Caring and Compassion

We appear to be teaching our potential leaders a model of leadership that is mechanistic, has defined 'right' and 'wrong' ways of doing things, is focused on money and treats human beings as resources to be hired and fired on a whim.

This is demonstrated in the BBC TV show *The Apprentice*, where each week candidates for a high powered and well paid job compete with each other to avoid being fired by Sir Alan Sugar. The show is based on the US Apprentice show featuring Donald Trump. Candidates are allocated to teams to complete a business-related task but, because one person from the losing team each week is fired, candidates often employ the strategies that further their own cause rather than those that best work for good of the team.

I don't, for one moment, believe that Sir Alan's approach on TV is the same as that he employs in his day to day business life. It is clearly exaggerated to create tension and thus entertainment. Sir Alan has been in business for many years and has built successful companies with loyal employees within them. The ruthless 'no excuses, fire 'em' approach he takes on the show wouldn't have helped him to do that. An example of this would be that, in a recent series of The Apprentice, the outright winner had openly lied on his CV and admitted the fact. When Sir Alan chose him as the series winner, it risked giving the impression that such an activity might be acceptable in business.

The problem is that a proportion of viewers believe that what they are watching is how business is actually conducted. So we get copycat 'Apprentices' arriving in business and thinking that they should play the same games with the same amoral attitude. Perhaps worse, we may miss out on the skills and talent of those who decide that business is simply not for them.

Most leadership is about people. Leaders need followers, people who believe in their vision and direction. History is littered with examples of leaders who abused the trust of their followers and led them into places they would never have gone alone. Leading with humanity is about developing a relationship of trust with your

Leaders **need** followers

followers and not abusing the position of power that they give you. I believe, and will explain why later in this book, that you need to love your team, even those who go out of their way to be unlovable.

The Entrepreneur Within

I have had a long and varied business career, so, in order to put a context for the rest of this book, I've set out my entrepreneurial journey in **Chapter 1**.

Leadership and entrepreneurship is about understanding what needs to be done and then doing it. It begins with ourselves and with taking action - for without action, nothing will ever happen. **Chapter 2** looks at taking action.

Our beliefs can nurture us and help us move forward or they can root us to the spot in fear - **Chapter 3** looks at our beliefs and how we can make them more helpful to us.

Chapter 4 widens the focus and looks at how we behave and succeed when leading a team.

The ultimate team is your own company. **Chapter 5** looks beyond the brand and marketing image and into the spirit and culture of a business and the role of a leader in developing and maintaining that.

Chapter 6 returns to the personal and looks at the importance of energy and health in our role as a successful leader. My journey to 'reverse the ageing process' is also examined here.

This book will give you information, inspiration and insights, increases your belief in yourself and your abilities and helps you to take successful action. If it does, I've achieved my goal.

1. My Entrepreneurial Journey

"Success is a journey, not a destination."

Arthur Ashe

It has been quite a challenge to summarise 73 years of my life and learning. I thought a lot about the value of doing this and I believe that the value is to demonstrate how despite my relatively lowly upbringing and my basic education, I was able to create an Academy for developing leaders and entrepreneurs. This chapter is the story of that journey.

I was born on the 18th October 1936, within the sound of the Bow Bells, which means that I am officially a Cockney. I am the eldest son *(of four)* born to Louis and Doris, who were children of immigrants from Poland and Russia.

Most of my formative years were during the Second World War, making my childhood very difficult. I was nine years old when the war ended and Lou was demobbed from the Royal Air Force. We moved to Margate in Kent where my parents ran a hotel. My education was very mixed. I went to several schools and I did not do well. I believe, in recalling this time, that I was a late developer. I left school at 14½ years of age, six months before the legal age at that time, as Lou and Doris moved back to London while Lou struggled to find a career. I was never pushed at school and I had no inclination to go on to college.

At the age of 15, I took my first job working for a certified accountant in the City of London at 21 shillings a week *(just over £1 – a shilling being the same as 10p)*. My travel costs were considerably more than that. I set about proactively educating myself by going to evening classes. Starting from such a low beginning, I never achieved anything at those classes. Lou and Doris then moved back to Margate and I moved with them. Once there I had a series of quite good jobs and always did well at whatever I did.

At the age of 17½, I volunteered to join the Royal Air Force, six months before I was legally required to join, as National Service was compulsory at that time. This was a totally proactive decision *(which I talk about elsewhere in the book)* and Lou and Doris were not even aware that I was going for interviews. Having successfully passed the examinations, the first I had ever passed, to join the Royal Air Force, my three years there were very influential in my character development. I volunteered for everything and started to pass small examinations and to manage other people, first in an office and later in Gibraltar, where I was responsible for furnishing the Officer's Married Quarters. I passed further exams which gave me the responsibility for armaments and other stores.

I left the Air Force at the age of 20½ and soon met my wife Jaclyn. I very quickly found a new job and started working for the John Lewis Partnership *(JLP)* at the Peter Jones store in Sloane Square, Chelsea , where I was singled out by the Managing Director, Lionel Wharrad. I started on the junior circuit and quite quickly began to manage various departments, becoming a rising star in the store. I studied and was awarded a diploma in design and interior decoration then, after three years, made the decision to move to Canada. Although I was with Jacky, she was unable to go with me. Within one day of arrival, I got a job in Toronto in a department store for one year.

Three months later, I returned to the UK to Jacky and to the Peter Jones store, where Lionel Wharrad was delighted to have me back. I was continually promoted and the experience was outstanding. My self esteem blossomed. I learnt how to manage staff and was very proud of being able to place people in their best roles. Developing people was *(and still is)* very important to me. The training that I got at the John Lewis Partnership was second to none. However after 5 years, Lionel Wharrad left and joined Booker Brothers, McConnell. He called me and asked me to join him there. They were starting up a group of departmental stores and Lionel wanted me to become a buyer for them. This was a wonderful opportunity which I took. After a while, Bookers bought a small group of retail shops and a food cash and carry. I was asked to manage the buying for the whole group. I had a very large department to run and was again a star in the organisation.

At the age of 30, Bookers sent me to Guyana and Trinidad as a consultant to the department stores there with a brief to come back with a plan to develop the stores in England.

Subsequent to this, Bookers decided to sell the organisation and offered me several internal jobs. Finally, I went with the small retail chain they had developed and joined up with Combined English Stores *(CES)* run by Murray Gordon. I worked with him as his trouble shooter as he bought several groups of stores. I was asked to appraise them before they were bought – quite something for someone at the age of 33!

After the wonderful culture of the John Lewis Partnership – especially the fact that all employees were partners - I found the culture of CES very disappointing and some policies were not in line with my business upbringing and philosophy. So I left and joined a smaller company that was about to go public. Initially, I was asked to join to bring some professionalism to the organisation. I became a Director of the company which was later floated on the Stock Market. I was firstly responsible for all the IT and had to learn as I introduced a large computer system into the organisation. The organisation then went into the food cash and carry business and I was asked to manage those. At the same time, I brought together 30 or 40 other cash and carries to form one of the largest food buying groups in the country called Landmark. A lot of my management skills and key beliefs in dealing with people fairly and openly were built during this period.

The holding company then got into financial difficulty and decided to sell the cash and carries which were by then up to 6 units. The holding company bought in a new chairman, Roy Garner, who certainly helped me to develop my own skills to a new level.

Roy eventually helped me to do a Management Buy Out *(MBO)* of two of the largest of the cash and carries. For the first time in my life, I had my own business and had to put into practice all my skills of leadership and management in order to build a good team. I was very successful for five years. However in 1981, the company overtraded through a series of unfortunate events and went into receivership. I learned a lot from my auditor, Colin Wagman, who helped me to structure the company in the way in which I did not lose everything. I was able to come out with some money and start a new cash and carry which I ran for three or four years before I sold it at a profit.

In 1983, I went into the video business which was growing at a great rate. When the cash and carry was sold I started to develop this business separately and began to develop concessions within many of the major stores and cash and carries around the country, building a very successful video film renting company. When this company needed more cash, I sold a shareholding to Hillsdown Holdings, which enabled them to develop the business. With Hillsdown, I sold this business successfully and, in doing so, I learned a lot about the workings of corporate financing. The company purchasing the business did not want me to continue in post but allowed me to work on an invention which I had been developing for vending rental videos and this carried on for a year or so.

I contacted the Department of Trade and Industry proactively and was given the opportunity to be a consultant for them, going round various businesses helping them to get grants from the DTI. This enabled me to see many, many companies and evaluate their needs and also see how successful the consultancies were that the DTI paid for. After a couple of years, it became clear to me that I could become a consultant in business management. I did this for a couple of businesses free of charge and then became recognised as a consultant with the DTI. I used my skills in identifying problems within businesses, which were usually around people and communication. I specialised in helping accountants and solicitors develop their organisations and achieved two or three notable successes in this area. I didn't enjoy the consultancy side as, with the DTI, it was the size of the report that mattered rather than the quality. This involved a lot of writing, which was not something I enjoyed.

An opportunity came up to join the UK operation of an American organisation called The Executive Committee *(TEC)* which developed leaders. I joined as chairman of a group and eventually became the top chairman within the organisation in the UK, running four groups, and won several awards from America for my work. After four years, I was asked to become managing director and it was something I really wanted. This was at the age of 59. The UK franchise holder then changed his mind and, after subsequent discussions, I decided to resign. The groups that I was very successfully running decided to help me to start up on my own, which, with the agreement of the franchise holder, I did. I then began building the Academy for Chief Executives.

The learning through the whole of this period has been profound, particularly when I reflect on the thousands of leaders that have passed through my hands. Many of them have become millionaires. As the whole business is dedicated to learning, I feel I have to be a model for that learning and therefore spend a lot of time on my own personal development. Even at my current age, I am still learning to bring value to people and I intend to continue doing that for many years to come.

The last two years have been very important to me as I feel that I am still delivering so much value to people and I want to carry on doing that. To this end I am learning a lot about health and wellness *(see more in Chapter 6)* which has resulted in my spending four weeks in India at the Jindal Naturecure Institute in Bangalore. I am learning how to avoid serious illness and, through yoga, diet and water, to 'reverse the ageing process'. I believe that I am now achieving that.

2. The Importance of Taking Action

*"Whatever you think you can do
or believe you can do, begin it.
Action has magic, grace,
and power in it."*

Goethe

Unless we take positive action for change, nothing will happen. It is one of my most basic beliefs and it has been reinforced in my work with hundreds of top executives where I have seen the difference that positive action can make.

Sometimes, we can feel blocked and unable to function and spend our time reflecting on what it is that is blocking us. This inertia can seem disabling and, as we spend more time thinking about it, completely impossible to overcome.

Motivation is a complex thing. Why we do one thing and not another can depend on many factors including our own self esteem, whether it seems to be worthwhile to do and our assessment of the consequences of not doing it.

We make choices all of the time. We can choose to sit and watch television. We choose to go out and do exercise. We choose to write a book. Why sometimes do we choose not to do anything? What creates that indecision or inertia, which will often ensure that we are not taking action and therefore are not achieving.

One theory suggests that we are motivated by two opposing forces - one 'towards' the possible benefits or the other 'away from' the potential consequences.

If we are operating in an 'away from' style, fear will play a part. Perhaps we fear that we will make a fool of ourselves or that we do not have the education.
We may also fear the taking of responsibility and of having ownership of anything we attempt to do. That fear may be fear of failure and ridicule but it may also be

the fear of success and of possibly standing out from the crowd, from our own friends and family. As Marianne Williamson put it, *"Our deepest fear is not that we are inadequate. Our deepest fear is that we are powerful beyond measure. It is our light not our darkness that most frightens us. We ask ourselves, who am I to be brilliant, gorgeous, talented and fabulous?"* [1]

It is this fear that may explain why some of us 'self sabotage'. Instead of doing what we know we can do and what we believe to be the right thing, we choose to do nothing or to engage in displacement or destructive activities.

What some may term as laziness, is simply a choice where doing nothing has more subjective value than doing something. Only our choices prevent us from being the best that we know we can be.

Motivation, or lack of it, is not the only barrier to taking action and achieving our goals. We might also be prevented from doing so by the culture of which we are part and the messages we have been given whilst growing up.

Being enthusiastic, studying and appearing to be clever are all things that those around you may have discouraged when you were young. Your parents may have been part of this learning process. Your school friends almost certainly were. It takes courage and belief to rise above such conditioning but it is possible and it may lead to achievement.

Let us examine one of the pieces of learned 'wisdom' that is worth challenging. Many of us were taught by our parents never to volunteer. But why should we not volunteer? If we don't volunteer, so the advice goes, we won't get into trouble. If we don't volunteer, we won't end up with more work than we want. This may be a well-meaning sentiment from people that care about us and don't want us to get hurt. They are worried that we don't know what we are getting ourselves into and they want to protect us. Perhaps they are concerned that if we take on too much, we will become overwhelmed or that others could take advantage of us. In extreme cases, we might experience 'burnout' due to the stress of too much work, too many extra responsibilities. It may also be a way of ensuring that we don't get 'above ourselves'.

As a young man, I signed up early for National Service and joined the Royal Air Force. National Service was compulsory for all young men and, at the age of

[1] **Marianne Williamson from *A Return To Love: Reflections on the Principles of A Course in Miracles*, Harper Collins, 1992**

seventeen and a half, they would be 'called up' for service and allocated to one of the Armed Services. Because I volunteered before my 'call up' was due, I was able to choose the service I joined and was able to better enhance my career and life. It was an early lesson for me that it is good to volunteer. That was, for me, the start of a better future.

I have not been trained as a psychologist; however, I have learned to observe my own behaviour and that of other people over many years. I was also taught this 'never volunteer' philosophy at a very young age and practiced it for many years, until one day I realised I needed to change. I wanted more and I saw that I needed to take action. I needed to build new relationships and I needed to believe that I was good enough.

So let's change the dynamic to a positive one. What would happen if we always volunteered, if we were always positive with every action that we took? I wonder how that would open the world for us and allow us to achieve our visions, our dreams. It is important therefore to move from a position of negative thought to a position of positive thought. It is a simple process and requires belief. What do you need to do to change negative thoughts into positive thoughts? What would you need to do to believe that this is possible?

Here are two exercises to do which will prove beyond any doubt how positive thought creates the positive action that leads to achievement.

Positive thought *creates the*
Positive action *that leads to*
achievement

Exercise 1 – *a Big Stretch*

Stand with your feet slightly apart. Just relax and put your right arm out in front of you. Turn it to the right as far as you can go and note the spot where your finger can stretch to. Then come back to the front. Relax; shut your eyes and picture where you were able to turn to, where your finger was pointing to. Just start to think positively of how much further your finger could go. Think of a spot that is 50% further than where you got to. Feel it, think it and see it. Say to yourself

'I will go 50% past my mark – I will do it easily.'

With that vision clear in your mind, keeping your eyes closed, put your arm out in front of you and turn to your right again as far as you can go. I am sure you have gone further than you had before - maybe 50% and maybe more!

Exercise 2 – *Wakey, Wakey*

This is an exercise which not only shows how extraordinary your mind is, but how much you can influence what happens to you through self talk. I have practiced this for years and do not remember where I first heard it. However I recently read it again in a book called *Goal Mapping* by Brian Mayne[2].

When I go to bed I think of the time I want to wake up in the morning. If I assume this is 6.00am, I will then bang my head six times on the pillow and say to myself **one, two, three, four, five, and six** and sure enough I will wake up at 6.00am. Now be even subtler. Suppose I want to wake up at 6.15am. Then I bang my head on the pillow six times and then say **'a quarter'** and sure enough I will wake up at 6.15am. Test it out. Set your alarm clock to wake you 5 or 10 minutes after you have told yourself to wake up. You will be surprised how accurate you will be!

These exercises will clearly change your belief. They will change your view that you can do anything you want to do. You have the power within you to do it. You need to understand what this power within you really is.

Often the fears that prevent you from acting are not real, just a story that you tell yourself. You don't have to tell that story. If you can find out where it is coming from, you can overcome it. If you can replace 'away from' motivation with more 'towards' ideas, you will find that it is easier to be motivated. That involves setting goals.

---

[2]*Goal Mapping: How to Turn Your Dreams into Realities* by Brian Mayne, Watkins Publishing (19 Jan 2006)

One of the things I do, and encourage others to do, is to set different types of goals.

This works by setting **5 goals** in each of the following categories.

- **Business**
- **Personal**
- **Charitable**

goals

To ensure those goals are in alignment with your vision and that they are challenging yet achievable, use the **SMART** approach. In this approach, each goal will be **S**pecific, **M**easurable, **A**chievable, **R**ealistic and **T**ime Based. The more you work on each aspect of the goal, especially on being realistic and setting target dates for each goal, the more you will begin to develop a winning habit of making and delivering goals.

Goals are useful as an internal device for motivating yourself, but they are so much more powerful when shared. Once you have set goals, tell people about them. You will be surprised how people will react once they know what your goals are and how they will often help you, how they will want you to succeed.

Take your goals and take ownership of them. Only you can achieve them. Only you have the responsibility to do this. Nothing can stop you achieving, providing you take the responsibility and don't blame others. Remember that we all have the choice to do whatever we want to do. Anything we don't do is not because someone else told us not to do it or because we were "too busy" or because something else happened. We didn't do it because we chose not to do it.

We **always** have **choice**

Sometimes we blame our motivation. The way to deal with that is to take small steps, not large ones. David Allen, in his book *Getting Things Done*[3] talks about the difference between a sub- project and an action. If the item you place on your 'To Do' list is too big, or you can't easily work out how it can be done, the chances are that you won't do it. Instead, it will remain on your action list for a long time and generate negative feelings of guilt whenever you think about it. What better way to self sabotage?

The use of the SMART acronym has not been attributed as there is considerable uncertainty over its origins.

[3]*Getting Things Done: The Art of Stress-Free Productivity,* **David Allen, Penguin (Non-Classics) 2002**

Goals are best couched in positive language. You might have told your children not to do something - not to turn the television on, not to drop the cup, for example. As soon as you tell them not to do something, they are more likely to do it. They will turn on the television, they will drop the cup – this is because we have put the thought into their minds. Instead of saying 'don't watch television', you might say 'play with a game whilst we are waiting to eat'. Instead of saying 'don't drop the cup' you might say 'are you enjoying that drink now?' The same approach can be used with your team at work.

*As you **get into the habit** of looking at everything **positively**,*
good things will happen around you

I'm sure you'll be able to think about examples of this within your own experience and, maybe, your own business. Being proscriptive can often produce results that are the opposite of those you wanted. Giving permission and encouragement will motivate those around you to achieve the results you do want and some you didn't expect.

Keeping your goals **SMART** and creating a habit of progressing and achieving your goals – as an individual and as a business – will result in the development of a virtuous circle and an attitude of success.

Specific

Measurable

Achievable

Realistic

Time Based

Well Formed Outcomes

In the early 1990s, I began to study NLP with Sue Knight who was a member of one of my Chief Executive Groups. In her book, NLP at Work, she talks about the difference between thinking based on the problems facing you and thinking based on desired and possible outcomes. I prefer outcome thinking.

In NLP a well-formed outcome is one that, as far as possible, meets the following basic conditions:

- **It is stated in the positive** *(that is, what you want, rather than what you don't want),*

- **It can be represented in the sensory systems so that it can be evidenced through the senses when attained.**

- **It should be possible and achievable.**

- **You have all the resources (people, psychophysiological states, time, capital, equipment, or material) required or accessible.**

- **It has a defined time frame.**

- **It must be 'ecological'. You should consider the costs and consequences for yourself and any others who are affected and be sure that they are acceptable according to your values and principles.**

There is much more about how to create well-formed outcomes in Sue's excellent book[4] and I recommend that to you.

Risk

Once you have your outcomes and goals clear, you move to taking action to achieve them. The most desirable outcomes often involve risks.

I can remember when I was about fourteen or fifteen years old and at a dance, sitting down but really wanting to ask a pretty girl across the room to dance. I could not bring myself to do it. I did not have the courage. I had a huge fear of her slapping me round the face or, even worse, ignoring me and then going to dance with someone else. All of my imagined outcomes were negative which totally destroyed the power within me to take action. Some of my friends seemed to have no problem asking girls to dance and they spent the night on the dance floor, not at a dusty table across the room. I believe that they may have also felt the

⁴NLP at Work by Sue Knight, (Nicholas Brealey Publishing; 3rd Edition - 2009)

fear of rejection but they acted despite this. They got the girls. Because I let fear take over, all I got was more and more miserable. I rejected myself! After a few times, I didn't even go to the 'stupid' dances.

Today, I look at opportunities much more positively. When networking for new business, I will take a positive view of the opportunities that could arise if a person found what I had to say was interesting. To take action, you have to start loving yourself. You have to start to recognise that you have value; that your glass is half full and not half empty.

I remember the fear I had when I took a group of Chief Executives to experience 'horse whispering'. This was a risky decision yet it still reverberates within my organisation as one of the most exciting events we undertook. By the end of the day we were all able to get a rapport with the horses to such a level that we could walk with them, run with them and trot with them at will. It became a metaphor for us all that we could go where angels fear to tread.

Think of the greatest achievers you know. People who achieve take action in every part of their lives. They take responsibility and ownership for what they do. They share their goals, their challenges and their dreams with others. By taking small steps and believing they can achieve, they do achieve.

By talking positively to yourself, you will start to achieve things totally beyond your expectations.

> *Successful people take action wherever they are, whenever the opportunity arises*

You might want to apply this to some aspect of your business where you know you could be doing so much more. Pretty much every business I've worked with has some areas that they would like to improve but nothing ever seems to happen. What is the worst thing that might happen if you were to take the risk? What might the benefit be if the risk pays off in full? Is the risk something that you are prepared to countenance in order to get the benefit? What about getting half the benefit? I'd strongly advise against 'betting the company' in one go, but making progressive moves, each with a risk that can be managed, could get you just as far.

Earlier, I talked about blaming a lack of 'motivation' for not achieving what we desire and I mentioned David Allen and his book *Getting Things Done*. Use his techniques to create projects that can be split into sub projects and then can be further divided into simple actions and start making changes one step at time. Who knows what changes may result?

One result of creating small tasks is that most of us have to do lists. They are often long and frequently have a lot of time invested in creating and maintaining them. As the week progresses and the to-do list gets longer, you may find that you become disappointed and frustrated as you find you are unable to complete every task on the list. Perhaps a feeling of futility overcomes you, too, as you realise that you simply cannot complete it. Maybe you know that feeling.

The temptation to do everything and make sure that nothing is missed can lead to items appearing on the list that are simply not worth the effort of recording, let alone doing or which could be done equally well by others in the organisation. Maybe, as well as adding to your to do list, you also keep hold of magazines and reports which you'll read 'when I have time'. Now is the time to let go.

Our ability to hold items in short term memory is limited. George A Miller – in 1956 - suggested that we could store 7 ± 2 items, though Wikipedia notes that more recent study suggests that 4-5 items is more realistic[5] . The more irrelevant the material we try to process, the more confused and frustrated we become. To overcome memory overload, you need a 'let go list'.

They work together. There will be items on your to do list that don't need doing at all – drop them - and items where others can do the task as well or better than you can yourself - delegate them. If you are unlikely to read all of those journala, articles, papers etc. that are retained 'for reading', pass them on to someone who will read them and maybe use the information to your benefit or simply put them in the recycling bin.

[5]**http://en.widipedia.org/wiki/George_Armitage_Miller**

Recently, I became a vegetarian for no other reason than to establish that I could do it. The inspiration to do it came from reading the book The Monk who Sold his Ferrari by Robin S Sharma[6] - His theory is that if you do something for 21 days it will be habit forming. Achieving the goal gave me far more than just a change of diet. Rather than seeing it as a negative – giving up meat – I chose to see it as the cultivation of a new habit of eating – something with a positive outcome. Giving up a habit is far easier when it is replaced by acquiring a better habit.

So my challenge to you is this. Undertake to give up something for 21 days and see what transformation it will bring into your life. The habit you choose to lose may be business or personal and it will probably be something that you know (though may not admit) is holding you back. What might it be for you? Write it down and then find a better habit with which to replace it.

Once you have done this once, you may find that it, in itself, becomes a habit. As we travel through our daily lives we accumulate habits and activities that once were useful but are now no longer needed or could be done in different ways. Getting rid of this accumulation allows you to simplify and focus.

Leadership and management should begin with our own cluttered lives.

If you truly want to achieve more than you are currently achieving then you must plan, make decisions, change your beliefs and change what you do. Above all create a positive attitude to your life. Never give in to an 'I can't do' attitude. Change your language to a 'can do' attitude. Then become aware of the new energy that emanates from you and how that positively affects every part of your life. As you recognise this and record this in your mind your new awareness becomes a habit which leads to creation of achievements and fulfilments beyond your biggest dreams.

I have recently learnt that great leaders spend 75% of their time creating a culture that encourages their people to develop their strengths leaving only 25% for their weaknesses. Most of us reverse this procedure, spending far too much time on weaknesses, with the result that our people seldom achieve their full potential[7].

[6]*The Monk who sold his Ferrari*, **Robin S Sharma (Element Books;New edition 2004)**
[7]*Now, Discover Your Strengths; How to Develop Your Talents and Those of the People You Manage,* **Marcus Buckingham Donald Clifton (Pocket Books; New edition 2005)**

3.   You Become What You Believe

Action *and* **beliefs** *are* **interdependent**

When I started to write this book, I gave a lot of thought as to what comes first and decided that it was taking action. If you want to achieve you cannot unless you do something about it, unless you take positive action for change. However as I ponder this, I think that the first priority, the first thing you have to do, is to believe. I couldn't start this book; I couldn't take action until I was confident that I had enough information, perhaps enough style to actually write something meaningful. Positive action and beliefs are interdependent.

Received beliefs

We manage our lives through the structure of our beliefs. Our beliefs are nurtured from very early in our childhood, perhaps even when we are in the womb. Perhaps they are inherent in our genes, but, certainly, they get quite ingrained as we are growing up. Not only are our beliefs set by our own experiences, but we model them on other people's beliefs, people who we admire, people by whom we are taught – our parents, our siblings, our teachers, our friends and our mentors.

I live by two very strong behaviour beliefs taught to me by my father which are embedded in my psyche and if I don't act according to what he ingrained in me I feel very uncomfortable. They act as drivers for me every day.

The first belief is that I must never start eating at the dinner table until everybody has been served. Many times my food goes cold whilst I wait for the last person to be served. In some respects, it is a limiting belief but is important to me.

The second one is that when I walk down the street with a woman, I always walk on her outside. I recall as a child walking down the street with my mother and, if I wasn't on the outside, my father would keep elbowing me until I moved to the other side. Now, whoever I am walking with, my wife, my daughters or friends, I have to walk on the outside otherwise I am extremely uncomfortable.

Beliefs control our life

When I think about beliefs, I realise that our lives are controlled by them. The actions we take are based on some sort of belief which is built within us.
I have a friend who feels he was seriously cheated by a bank and by a set of his supporting accountants. He often says to me, *'I now no longer trust anybody'*. I cannot imagine a life where I don't trust people. I prefer to trust until I have been let down and, even then, I like to believe they have done the best they can.

One of my own beliefs is that wars are created by people who have strong limiting beliefs, often around religion, and the parties at war believe their truth is the only truth. These beliefs become fundamental to the point where they have to overcome the other side's beliefs and thus wars and killing become part of their lives. On a smaller scale, family conflicts also arise between people with different sets of beliefs that are fundamental to the way each lives.

So to be able to achieve positively, to be able to develop and improve relationships, to be able to sell your product or service, to be able to maintain your marriage, your friendship; you have to understand your own beliefs and what drives you.

Most of us cannot achieve all that we desire because we are held back by limiting beliefs.

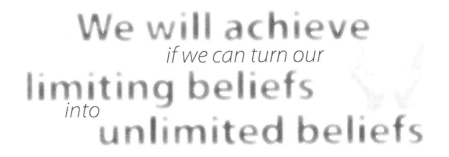

We will achieve *if we can turn our* limiting beliefs *into* unlimited beliefs

Exercise – *Limiting beliefs*

How do we change our limiting beliefs to unlimited beliefs?

The most interesting exercise that I have come across is one where you take a word such as **MONEY** or **SEX** or **SALES** and then write down all the beliefs you have around that word.

For instance MONEY

LIMITING BELIEF	UNLIMITED BELIEF
Money is the root of all evil	*Money is good*
Look after the pennies and the pounds will look after themselves	*All money is relevant*
Money is power	*Money is a measure*
Money speaks	*People speak*
Money buys happiness	*Happiness is a state of mind*
Money corrupts	*Money enables*
Time is money	*Time is priceless*
If you pay peanuts you get monkeys	*People work for people*
All people work for money	*People are all different*

Try and write **ten** of your own beliefs around sales. If you do it as a group exercise, it makes it even more interesting. The result will normally be a list of limiting beliefs. Then write down next to each item, a sentence that means the **exact opposite** – a sentence that represents the **unlimited belief** framed in a positive way.

When you write this list against your own limiting beliefs, you will be astonished at how that belief controls your view of the world and thus your destiny. If you want to change in a way that is truly transformational you will need to consciously change this belief to something which is unlimited.

Beliefs can help or hinder us when we move to action. When a footballer is preparing to take a penalty, he can think that he will miss or that the goalkeeper will save it. That becomes his belief and the chances are higher that he will miss. If he is able to truly believe that he will score, the chances are high that he will score.

A clear example of this was at a cricket test match in November 2006, between England and Australia. England had won the Ashes series in England for the first time in 20 years and this was the subsequent series being played in Australia. People were getting very hyped up. The main strike bowler from England bowled the first ball which went about 10 feet wide. Clearly the bowler froze, maybe overwhelmed by the occasion. Normally this would not be an issue and the next ball would be straight and strong but because it was so bad, his head went down and he lost belief in his ability to bowl at all so this brought him down and, with him, the rest of the team. They lost the match by a very serious margin and went on to lose the series.

As I approached the age of 70 I heard my friends, some of them considerably younger than myself, say things like *"I can't remember names", "I can't do this", "I can't walk any further"* and *"I can't do my job".* Their excuse was always that ***"I'm getting older".*** My unlimited belief is that I can do anything that I want to do and as I get older I can do it better, with more wisdom and more experience. There are many other excuses we use on a daily basis to avoid taking action. Whatever your excuse, you can always reframe it to overcome the belief and move forward.

There is now much written about how belief can positively impact on illness and has even changed a terminal illness into a new healthy state. Deepak Chopra, a qualified medical doctor, is a leading writer in this area. In a recent article he proposes that the mind can be its own placebo and bring about recovery based on belief. ***"But those who recovered against all odds did have one thing in common. At a certain point people who are inexplicably cured know that they are going to recover. Their doubts and fears lift. With great conviction they realize that they are no longer in danger. (To be clear, we are talking about a strong correlation, not a fact that applies to everyone.) This certainty is like becoming your own placebo. What would that mean?"***[8]

Brandon Bays in her book *The Journey* tells how she cured herself of a serious illness through her strong belief that she could. Brandon now runs courses on how to do this for yourself.[9]

Until recently I had only read about this but in the last few months a good friend of mine had breast cancer and at the point of having a mastectomy and chemotherapy, she decided to cure herself through positive thoughts and diet and she has succeeded.

[8] **http://deepakchopra.com/2010/02/how-to-be-your-own-placebo/**
[9] **The Journey: An extraordinary Guide for Healing Your Life and Setting Yourself Free by Brandon Bays (Thorsons; 1999)**

In 2007, I met a man who is 123, is able to speak 13 languages and is moving his yoga business back to India from New York. His secret is to believe he will live forever and also believes in being vegan. His name is Yogi Swami Bua Ji *(see Chapter 6 for more on my beliefs about ageing).*

Our mind is conditioned by what we believe and therefore if we change our belief, our conditioning changes and we behave and act differently. If we want to change behaviour, if we want to change a situation, if we want to change the world, the first thing to do is to change our state by changing our belief.

Exercise – *changing states*

We all face challenges and sometimes it is quite natural that we should feel overwhelmed or daunted by them. When we feel jaded or unable to face something that is critical but a real challenge, wouldn't it be good if there was something we could do to feel better equipped to cope?

There is - and it doesn't need anything other than you and your own experiences and resources. You can do it in the privacy of your office or you can do it in public - no one will be the wiser.

So what is this 'magic' technique? It is remarkably simple and very powerful for most people. I'd recommend giving it a try. It may seem a little strange at the outset but will soon become second nature.

The first stage is to decide how you want to feel. What resources might you need to deal with the issues that are facing you and maybe holding you back? Maybe you need patience or optimism or energy or clarity of thought or maybe you want to feel invincible? Whatever it is you need, choose one.

Let us choose energy.

Now stand, feet apart and in a relaxed posture and recall a time when you felt very energetic, when nothing could hold you back. Feel that feeling, see what you saw and hear what you heard at that time. As the feeling intensifies, touch your finger and thumb together or make some distinctive physical movement that you can repeat unobtrusively. You can now use that physical movement to recall that state and experience it again. This is called an *'anchor'.* You can create more anchors for other resources in the same way.

Try it and see what happens. If the state you achieve isn't powerful enough, try intensifying the recollection by making any images bigger and brighter, any sounds louder and any feelings more intense. The more you do this, the better the effect when you *'fire off'* the anchor.

Anchoring is just one element of Neuro Linguistic Programming *(NLP)*, a set of tools and techniques for achieving peak performance. As I mentioned, I learned these techniques from Sue Knight[10]. There are many business-based NLP trainers who can help you to learn more. For leaders, or anyone with a highly demanding job, I strongly recommend finding out more about its uses and effects. It may be the difference between being overtaken by events or turning them to your advantage.

If you **truly** *want to achieve something, however small or large, try to* **change your belief** *around it and you will find that you* **will** *get* **remarkable results**

When you start to understand yourself, when you recognize how your beliefs affect what you say, you will begin to understand others. This will help you to help others to achieve. As a leader, this is vital, as your beliefs can help or hinder overall team performance.

Unlimited beliefs

[10]www.sueknight.com

4. Leading a Team - *Tools and Habits*

> *"If your actions **inspire**
> others to dream more, learn more,
> do more and become more,*
> **you are a leader"**

John Quincy Adams

There is a popular perception that a leader is someone who is alone, aloof and self-sufficient; that the leader is someone who makes decisions and then makes everyone else follow them – perhaps by the sheer force of their personality. Whilst there may be such leaders, most leaders need other people to help them and support them to thrive and prosper.

In my view, leaders today need a number of competencies:

1. **They need to have a clear vision or purpose.**

2. **They need to have the ability to mentor, coach and develop people. Unless leaders are able to carry their people along with their vision and purpose then their business will ultimately fail.**

3. **The Leader today must also create an environment with a soul and a heart. People come to work for more than money and they need to have an environment that is nurturing and allows them to fulfil their potential.**

The leader should care to the point of loving their people. Even if it is regretfully necessary to fire them it should be done in such a way that the whole of the community understands that the reasons for doing it are right.

In my experience, the best leaders do at least one other thing well, they communicate. That communication is both internal –with their team and their backers – and externally, with those who can support them and help them on their mission.

A good leader consults before making a decision, takes into account all the advice he or she can find and then communicates the decision clearly and promptly once it is made. That decision is only good for the circumstances at the time of the decision, so the leader should then watch the feedback as the decision is implemented to identify and act upon changes that affect the course of action being taken. Decisions are never cast in stone and can be adjusted over time as circumstances change.

At The Academy for Chief Executives, we have identified the needs and wishes of business leaders –

- **Leaders need** *peers to talk to without conflicting interests*

- **Leaders need** *to refuel and replenish their own energy for growth*

- **Leaders need** *a supportive and challenging space to explore new ideas and solutions without feeling exposed or losing face*

- **Leaders learn** *through experience, so need access to practical models and concrete examples of how others deal with similar challenges. Immediacy of application is important*

- **Leaders need** *more rigour in tracking business performance*

- **Leaders wish** *to raise their aspirations about what they can have, what they can do and who they can be.*

Those things we provide through networking leaders together.

Teams and Leaders

The nature of teams is changing and, with that change, leaders themselves are also changing. Many leaders now lead virtual teams – sometimes across business boundaries – and they need to be leaders by consent and influence. Even for leaders who have direct team reports, this is a good model to follow. Leading by consent rather than coercion is always a good approach in my experience.

Being the team leader doesn't mean that you must be the leader in all circumstances. Sometimes, the really good leader has to step back and let someone else take control. Leadership depends on the requirement facing the team. Sometimes a lower level team member should be the leader simply because they have the necessary knowledge or skills to effectively resolve the situation.

Recognising this and providing the permission for it to happen are characteristics of a great leader.

Get a group of leaders together, as I often do, and ask them about their priorities in leading teams to successful achievement and you will get a number of different answers. Some will prioritise the task in hand and assume that everything will fall into place. For others it is about pulling together the right team with the right blend of people in it and for yet others, it will be about developing the individuals within the team.

So, with so much disparity on the topic, who is right? Actually, they all are, or at least each of the views is partly right. Good leaders concentrate on all three areas – the task, the team and the individual.

In my career I have been involved in retail, a business that depends on the individuals (often the lowest paid in the organisation) who meet the customers directly and on a daily basis. They are part of teams that may be responsible for a part of a department store or the complete chain store. Each team has a number of tasks, not least that of achieving customer satisfaction. Satisfied customers return and spend money with the retailer. A retail manager who leads a team to achieve that goal has to consider if the store has the right stock and the means of displaying it; or if it is clean, warm and welcoming, so customers will return. There has to be a team responsibility to manage stock and to ensure that it is merchandised on to the floor at appropriate times.

The better the team works together, the better the experience the customer gets and the more likely they are to feel welcomed in the store. The overall ambience of a store is something you may be able to detect within minutes of arriving. Whether you notice the atmosphere consciously or not, it will influence you. It will be positive, negative or just neutral and it will affect your state of mind and your feelings towards continuing to purchase or moving on to the next store.

So that's team and task. The role of the individual is the one you may recognise most readily. We have all experienced the good and the bad of customer service at some point in our lives. Whether it is someone having a bad day and simply ignoring or dismissing your needs, or someone who goes out of their way to find that item you've been searching for, or who takes the time to talk to you and understand your requirements properly, their attitude and approach make a significant difference to your response to that store, to the company and to their brand.

The best store in the world will fail if the staff they employ give a poor or offhand service to their customers or if the store is simply untidy and unwelcoming or if it has the wrong stock or is badly merchandised. Retail leadership is as much about detail as it is about strategy. The top retail leaders spend as much time as they can in their stores and getting close to their staff and customers.

Your business may not be retail but the same need for detail and for the three pronged approach to leadership that John Adair, one of the world's leading authorities on leadership and leadership development, developed, is probably just as true. There are three balls in the air – dare you drop any of them?

Each person that you lead will have different needs and your approach should be different. Their needs will also differ across time and as they tackle new or unfamiliar roles. So it is important to know where they are developmentally and apply the appropriate leadership style.

Paul Hersey and Kenneth Blanchard, developer of the *One Minute Manager* series of books, created a model for situational leadership[11] in the late 1960's. It allows you to analyse the needs of the situation you're dealing with, and then adopt the most appropriate leadership style. There are four leadership styles in Hersey and Blanchard's model and four sets of circumstances. As with any model, this is highly granular and needs interpreting by the leader as they approach a given situation.

Leadership

Teams and Leaders

More on John Adair and Action Centred Leadership at http://www.johnadair.co.uk/
[11]**The ideas in this section are based on those set out in the book *Leadership and the One Minute Manager* (1985) by Kenneth H. Blanchard, Patricia Zigarmi, and Drea Zigarmi which is still available in a 2000 edition. There are several websites that summarise this work including –**
http://www.chimaeraconsulting.com/sitleader.htm
http://en.wikipedia.org/wiki/Situational_leadership_theory
http://changingminds.org/disciplines/leadership/styles/situational_leadership_hersey_blanchard.htm
Ken Blanchard has, apparently moved on to a new Situational Leadership Model (known as Situational Leadership® II (SLII)) whilst Paul Hersey continues to develop this original model. Read more at –
http://www.situational.com/ for Hersey's work and
http://www.blanchardtraining.com/solutions/onetoone/sl2/ for SLII

The approach of a team member *(or follower)* is represented by two factors, competence and commitment. The four combinations that the model suggests are important are –

- **D4** High Competence and High Commitment

  Experienced at the job, and comfortable with their own ability to do it well. May even be more skilled than the leader.

- **D3** High Competence and Variable Commitment

  Experienced and capable, but may lack the confidence to go it alone, or the motivation to do it well / quickly

- **D2** Some Competence and Low Commitment

  May have some relevant skills, but won't be able to do the job without help. The task or the situation may be new to them.

- **D1** Low Competence and Low Commitment

  Generally lacking the specific skills required for the job in hand, and lacks any confidence and / or motivation to tackle it.

You may recognise that, as a leader, you also fall into one of these categories depending on the role you are playing. Some entrepreneurs who operate with High Competence (D4) when doing deals, find themselves with little of no competence *(and sometimes little commitment) (D1 or D2)* when it comes to administration or VAT returns, with the result that these are tasks that they, rightly in my view, delegate elsewhere. Delegation is one of the four leadership styles available –

- **Directing Leaders** *define the roles and tasks of the 'follower', and supervise them closely. Decisions are made by the leader and announced, so communication is largely one-way.*

- **Coaching Leaders** *still define roles and tasks, but seeks ideas and suggestions from the follower. Decisions remain the leader's prerogative, but communication is much more two-way.*

- **Supporting Leaders** *pass day-to-day decisions, such as task allocation and processes, to the follower. The leader facilitates and takes part in decisions, but control is with the follower.*

- **Delegating Leaders** *are still involved in decisions and problem-solving, but control is with the follower. The follower decides when and how the leader will be involved.*

I'm sure you will be beginning to see how the theory works. Leaders need to develop the flexibility to operate in all of the four ways according to the situation of the follower.

The numbering system indicates the most appropriate combinations –

- **D4** High Competence *and* High Commitment *is ideal for a Delegating style (S4).*

- **D3** High Competence *and* Variable Commitment *probably requires a Supporting style (S3).*

- **D2** Some Competence *and* Low Commitment *indicate a need to develop both confidence and commitment and a Coaching style (S2) is the best fit for this.*

- **D1** Low Competence *and* Low Commitment *are most often found amongst new employees and temporary staff. It is also found when employees find themselves in a new role and change from being a very confident and motivated D4. The directive style (S1) is suggested by the model for this category, but I would urge leaders to move to a Coaching style just as soon as they can.*

One of the most important presuppositions of Neuro Linguistic Programming (NLP) is that 'the map is not the territory'. It is true here.

*A **model** is only useful as a guideline and **flexibility** is the **most important** principle to apply*

People do not neatly fit into four boxes and their needs are never met simply by one of four approaches. Depending who the person is and what their personal circumstances are, you may see changes in their performance that require changes in your approach. Working with empathy and healing is a good guiding principle *(more in a few pages)*. However, having a model like this is a simple way to know where and how to start with the leadership of an individual team member – and it reminds us all that to try and lead a team rather than individuals is a mistaken approach. Only when we lead the individuals in an optimum way can a team begin to emerge.

I believe that leaders should consider themselves to be providers of service to those who follow them. Robert Greenleaf wrote *(in a 1970 essay[12])* about the concept of Servant Leadership and it is one that I find to be in line with my own principles. Leaders lead not for their own benefit but for the benefit of those who are led by them.

Does that make them less of a leader? No, I don't think it does. Unless you are able to do everything yourself *(in which case you are probably not a leader anyway)*, you will need other people to deliver your visions and goals. If those people are treated well – as human beings – they are more likely to deliver.

Greenleaf, in Servant as Leader, makes a distinction between leaders who are servant first – *"it begins with the natural feeling that one wants to serve"* – and leaders first. *"Between them are shadings and blends that are part of the infinite variety of human nature"*. So there is no dogma here, no requirement to fit into a predetermined mould. Greenleaf proposes a test, which he acknowledges is difficult to administer, *"do those served grow as persons; do they while being served, become healthier, wiser, freer, more autonomous, more likely themselves to become servants?"*

[12]**http://www.greenleaf.org/whatissl/**

Being a servant doesn't strip the leader of authority, or make it less possible to achieve their goals. They are not servile leaders. Nelson Mandela has transformed South Africa through servant leadership. Larry Spears, CEO of the Greenleaf Centre has identified 10 characteristics of the Servant Leader[13] –

Listening – *"the servant leader seeks to identify the will of the group and helps to clarify that will."*

Empathy – *"the servant leader strives to understand and empathise with others".*

Healing – *"servant leaders recognise that they have an opportunity to help to make whole those with whom they come into contact"* *I will cover this thought in more detail a further article.*

Awareness – *"Able leaders are usually sharply awake and reasonably disturbed (in that they are out of their comfort zone). They are not seekers after solace. They have their own inner serenity."*

Persuasion – *"a reliance on persuasion rather than on one's positional authority, in making decisions within an organisation."*

Conceptualisation – *"servant leaders are called to seek a delicate balance between conceptual thinking and a day to day approach."*

Foresight – *"enables the servant leader to understand the lessons from the past, the realities of the present and the likely consequences of a decision for the future."*

Stewardship – *"assumes first and foremost commitment to serving the needs of others."*

Commitment to the growth of people – *"the servant leader recognises the tremendous responsibility to do everything in his or her power to nurture the personal and professional growth of employees and colleagues."*

Building Community – *"seeks to identify some means for building community among those who work in businesses and other institutions."*

[13]On Character and Servant - Leadership : Ten Characteristics of ...
http://chapters.ewb.ca/pages/president/leadership-articles-and-links/On%20Character%20
and%20Servant-Leadership.pdf

Servant leaders don't have to have all of these characteristics, but they all help to create the right atmosphere – the right culture – within an organisation. No- one is perfect but, by recognising the areas where we can improve, we begin to move ourselves forward. Servant leadership is not for everyone but I find it difficult to argue with any of the characteristics.

If a leader came along who displayed all ten, I'd be happy to be led by that person.

I will now focus in on two of those ten characteristics – Empathy and Healing. On first reading, these characteristics may seem to have less to do with good leadership than clarity and decision making and other leadership traits but, I believe, they are very important soft skills that really great leaders demonstrate in abundance.

Let me take empathy first. Empathy is the ability to put yourself in the position of the person to whom you are speaking and to understand them better. To Spears, empathy implies that you accept the person but can, if you need to, *"refuse to accept certain behaviours or performance".* This is an important differentiation that many otherwise good leaders occasionally forget. In football, it would be termed *"playing the ball, not the man".* Empathy may be a soft skill, but it does not imply softness in the performance that the team accepts. It is possible to empathise entirely with a team member whilst being engaged in a disciplinary process because it is the behaviour or performance that is at issue.

From time to time, you will come across members of your team who have, in Greenleaf's terms, *"broken sprits and have suffered from a variety of emotional hurts. Although this is part of being human, servant leaders recognise that they have the opportunity to help make whole those with whom they come in contact."* By terming this an 'opportunity', Greenleaf implies that the leader should see this as a service he wants to provide rather than a chore to be gone through because it has to be. This 'helping to make people whole' is what Spears terms 'healing'. He does not imply by this that you need to become a medical doctor. Medical conditions will not be cured by your actions, though they can be made infinitely easier to bear by a helpful and concerned attitude. No, what I believe is meant here is that you as a servant leader must take responsibility for the welfare of the team. As broken spirited or emotionally hurt team members can, and usually do, perform less well than their colleagues, there is a bottom line reason for doing this, too, though this should not be the driver.

Are you equipped to be a servant leader? Not everyone has active listening skills or a natural empathy and being able to help people to handle emotional issues takes skill and practice. However, there is almost certainly a basis on which to build your personal skills through training and mentoring. Not that you need to do it alone. Encouraging these attitudes, especially by example, throughout the company, will, even in the medium term, result in a happier and better performing team that works for, as well as with, each other. In business, soft skills can produce hard results.

In his book *Good to Great[14]*, *(Random House Business Books 2001)* based on a long running research project into what factors turned good performing companies into great performers, Jim Collins identified a type of leader he named **Level 5** leader. *"Level 5 leaders channel their ego needs away from themselves and into the larger goal of building a great company. It's not that Level 5 leaders have no ego or self-interest. Indeed, they are incredibly ambitious – but their ambition is first and foremost for the institution, and not themselves".*

The research team found that the leaders of Good to Great *(GTG)* companies were not high profile; in fact many of them were unknown outside of their own industry despite running highly successful companies. They had a paradoxical mixture of personal humility and a strong professional will. The term 'Level 5' came because such leaders top a hierarchy of leadership types and because the team couldn't find a suitable epithet to describe their mix of humility and determination.

Many **'big personality'** leaders are Level 4. The levels in the book are –

> **Level 1** – *Highly Capable Individuals*
>
> **Level 2** – *Contributing Team Member*
>
> **Level 3** – *Competent Manager*
>
> **Level 4** – *Effective Leader*
>
> **Level 5** – *Level 5 Executive*

Collins and the team identified some key attributes for **Level 5** –

- **Level 5 leaders** *set up their successors to succeed whereas Level 4 leaders can set up successors to fail and may also stay in post after their effectiveness has waned.*

- **Most (9 from the 11) Level 5 leaders** *came from inside the business. None of the 11 had high profile leaders bussed in from outside.*

[14]**http://www.jimcollins.com/article_topics/articles/good-to-great.html**

Collins remarks on the "irony ... that Boards of Directors frequently operate under the false belief that they need to hire a larger-than-life, egocentric leader to make an organisation great."

- *Collins also remarks on the mirror and window differences between Level 4 and Level 5. Level 5 leaders tend to look out of the window to find the reasons for success and look in the mirror to understand reasons for failure. Level 4 leaders tend to look in the mirror for the reasons they succeed and to blame external events and people for their failures.*

Are you a Level 5 leader?

- **Are you I or we oriented?**

  When talking about business achievements which pronoun do you most use? Did I implement the successful policy or did we?

- **Do you develop successors to be able to succeed not fail?**

  Have you a succession plan in place? Do those who will succeed you inherit a business in good running order or a potential wreck? Will it please you if the business falters without you at the helm?

- **Are you fanatical about the results your business achieves?**

  When the business succeeds do you give praise to 'the team' or take it all yourself? Who do you blame when things don't work out? Team, external factors or you?

- **When the going gets tough what do you do?**

  Stay the course and fight for the business? Find a way to get out, preferably with a nice payoff? Hide your head in the sand or confront the situation?

In the book, Jim Collins suggests that you don't obsess on this as it is not the only criterion for GTG and maybe not even the main one. He suggests that if you follow the other ideas from GTG then you will become a Level 5 leader anyway. I cover some of the other ideas in the next chapter – about leading a company – as they are more applicable in that situation.

Leadership is important but what you lead your business to do is more important. Actions are crucial in the pursuit of greatness as is surrounding yourself with the right people – and getting rid of the wrong ones.

I know a lot of senior business people who consider themselves to be very good leaders but not as good at managing people and motivating them. Like any other skill, managing key people well can be learned and through practice mastered. One technique for doing that makes, in my experience, a large difference.

You probably schedule regular one to one meetings with your top team and sometimes those meetings won't happen. The real world gets in the way and nothing beats the adrenalin rush of crisis management. Don't let that happen. The first rule is simple, regular meetings must happen regularly. They may be weekly, fortnightly or monthly but they must happen regularly.

The second rule is that the agenda for those regular meetings, after the first, will always be the same. For the first meeting, your team member should come with a list of the actions they intend to take over the period before your next meeting. As you discuss them, letting the team member explain how and why they intend to achieve each task, offer help and support where you can.

For subsequent meetings, the team member brings two lists – the list from the previous period as well as the list for the next one. Not everything will have been done and some tasks will have been more difficult (and some easier) than expected. Use the previous list for learning and not to blame or accuse. Understand whether the team member is prone to over ambition or under achievement and coach him or her where needed. The aim should be that each new list is stretching but not impossible and that it is relevant to the objectives of the company. Over time, you will find you need to say less as your team member comes up with his/her own solutions and insights.

Once it works for the top level, encourage team members to try it with their own direct reports. Then just watch the motivation happen – not from any Shakespearean speeches and exhortations but from within the teams themselves.

Networking is an important skill for business leaders and networking generally can lead to all sorts of benefits in business as new suppliers, advisers and advocates emerge. It may also prove to be the shortest distance between jobs. A friend was made redundant from his job as CEO in a large company. He called on his network for help and after a few conversations and lunches had built a database of over 1,000 people who might be able to help him. He found a new job within 10 days. Had he been looking for a business idea or opportunity, I'm convinced he would have found one.

Networking is not new as an activity. It happens everywhere and we often do it without realising that we are networking. We meet someone on a train, or in a café or hotel and the conversation often begins with what you do. We are pattern-seeking beings, so we soon start noticing similarities in our views or situations and we find that ideas can flow, or we find nothing much of interest in each other and move on. Sometimes we pursue these ideas and sometimes we don't. A lot of networking is very random – though it needn't be.

Where it gets organised a little more is where communities of interest begin to develop and people find that they get on with other members and begin, maybe, to do some business with each other or even create a business together. Business has been done over coffee for many years. It is how the insurance markets around Lloyd's of London began. Many other businesses have begun in the same way over the years.

Trade associations and trade exhibitions also provide ample opportunity to network and to keep abreast of or even ahead of, the changes in your industry. Such organisations are beginning to offer networking opportunities as part of their member benefits.

These days, the coffee is often being consumed by people who are miles apart and yet in close contact. They are using the internet to communicate, using one of the many tools that are available. I have Skype installed and can call people over the internet and, using a simple webcam, talk to them eye to eye. Encountering people, who may have similar interests or complementary skills, can also be done online. The generation that is joining businesses at the moment from college, is very familiar with online networking at sites like Facebook and MySpace. Younger people use Bebo to connect and share interest and views. Sites like LinkedIn provide opportunities for businesspeople to connect online, to communicate with each other with the ultimate aim of finding ways to do business together. My personal favourite site is Ecademy, a social network for business people, where anyone who subscribes can start a group on any topic and recruit members for it. This approach of networks within networks works for me and I have met many good people through it.

Leaders may not be lonely but they are alone, especially when it comes to making major decisions. When you aren't able to confide in even your closest colleagues within the business, you may need to have people externally who you know and trust to give you advice and support. Organisations like the Institute of Directors ought to be a good place to find such people, but of their approximately seventy thousand members, only about five thousand are Chief Executives or Managing Directors. Networking to find a reference group of other chief executives is not so easy.

There are organisations that are set up to make this possible, though. Vistage, the Young Presidents Association and my own Academy for Chief Executives, for example, can make it easier for you to find yourself new people who understand your role and the nature of the problems it throws up and can offer support when you need it – as you will when they need it.

If you are shy and don't like approaching people in networking meetings, try my approach. I simply stand quietly in the room and I find that people come to me. You don't have to be an extrovert or gregarious to network. But you do have to network.

Networking is about giving in order to be able to receive. The give comes first. At the Academy, I see a lot of people join for business reasons. They want to improve their business and gain an understanding of others' businesses. They do want to share ideas, but perhaps they don't realise what they are really going to get. New members usually start off quite slowly, not sharing very much, more observing. Gradually, through spending time with like-minded people, they open up more and more, and they find that they also have a lot to give: time, advice, opinions, an ear. All of a sudden their lives truly begin to open up. They originally joined for business reasons and they get friendship, trust, invaluable support and a whole lot more.

So spend your time giving. It doesn't matter what you join, just join something aligned with your interests.

Give opportunities to people. Join interest groups and give of your knowledge and information. Work with charities. Give your time and you will be surprised how this continues to ensure that you get fulfilment and achievement in everything you do.

Sharing of yourself is a key element here. The more you share ideas with friends and family – and even business contacts – the more it comes back to you. It creates an even stronger commitment to yourself and others in the process. Over dinner with my family during one of our holidays, I shared my intention to write this book. It was a scary moment and I felt very vulnerable, but I wanted them to know about something that was important to me. What I hadn't counted on was the total involvement and encouragement they would provide. My youngest grandson Dan really captured the vision. He asked if I had come up with a title, to which I said 'no'. He then told me he had a great idea for the title. And he would let me have it if I gave him ten percent of the proceeds! After I stopped laughing, I got out my notebook and wrote out a 'contract'.

Working towards achievement

As the leader of a team, it is your role to take the team in directions that they may not understand or want to take. It is your vision that chooses the route but it is the other people in the team who will determine whether the vision is turned into reality for you. So how do you take your vision and inspire your people to take action towards achieving it?

Even experienced leaders occasionally doubt their ability to turn vision into action. It only gets harder as the company grows and there are more people to be convinced and inspired to make the big ideas work. So, one of the first questions may be *'how do I get this proposal taken seriously?'* Having people outside the team that you can depend upon for advice, or with whom you can talk through a proposal, is an invaluable resource. They can help you to frame the vision in a way that allows others to buy into it.

It is your team so why can't you just tell everyone else how you want it to be and discipline those who don't comply? Whilst decisions can be imposed on the team, it is usually much more sensible to persuade rather than impose. Persuasion may come in waves. First external entities like the Board need to be convinced and then it can be cascaded down through management or it may be that the workforce has to be consulted to ensure that the proposal is workable. You may have trade unions to convince, as well. However you choose to do it, your homework needs to be properly done and the proposal communicated in a clear and compelling way. We all respond to stories and turning the proposal into a story can make it much easier to sell.

From recent publicity about climate change, it is clear that far more people are aware of, and generally understand, the problems but a small proportion of those are taking action to change the situation. The others probably haven't yet realised how it affects them directly. So it is for business change. Unless people see where they fit and how their contribution brings benefit – to the business and to themselves – they are unlikely to take intelligent action.

And intelligent action is what we need.

Most of us probably feel that meetings are a necessary evil and dream of the day when actions happen without all the sidetracks and rambles that meetings often take. Whether a meeting is between two people or a full board meeting of a dozen or more, there are ways to make sure that the meeting is effective in getting things done.

The secret is obvious once you know it, but I find so many leaders simply don't find the time to implement it even when they know it. They find themselves in a cycle of meetings which goes on for too long. As a result they arrive for subsequent meetings unprepared and so the cycle continues with overlong meetings blending into each other.

We all know that a meeting needs an agenda but a good agenda is focused and makes it clear to all concerned in the meeting just what the outcome of the meeting is intended to be. The leader needs to have a clear outcome from the meeting and needs to make it clear upfront. The outcome may be a decision on an issue facing the team or to achieve a common understanding or to approve a proposal but the simpler the outcome, the more effective the meeting can be. If every meeting was effective, just think how much time might be released and how much clarity there would be about the eventual outcome. Meetings could be halved in duration yet be so much more powerful in driving the business forward in a common direction.

Meetings are crucial *to all teams and businesses.*

The **more effective** *they are, the* **more effective** *the team and the business will be*

Action also needs to be timely. When a person has been employed, often in a highly-paid executive position, in a role for which they are unsuited, they often do not recognise that changes are needed or defer making change because they fear confrontation. They do not take action early enough and, as a result, the problem they were facing becomes more difficult and costly to resolve.

As leaders, we can get complacent and fail to see the obvious that is facing us daily. The environment where people work can get tired and shabby yet it is tolerated for far too long. This failure to take action is a detriment to the business. So why don't more people take positive action? What is it that causes them to lack motivation?

Getting better performance

Until I attended a 6-day course on Facilitation Mastery, I believed the most important competency or tool for the leader was the ability to coach. Darren Rudkin's[15] unique course on how to be a world-class facilitator changed that belief.

All 12 attendees now realise that coaching – and mentoring - is a part of facilitation. The challenge in facilitation is to hold the energy of a group of people and yet to focus on individuals to get the messages through. Darren used his considerable learning in this subject as one of the founding directors of *"What IF"* perhaps the most successful innovation and creative company the UK has produced.

Leaders spend as much as 95% of their time facilitating in one form or another in meetings of one or many people. By understanding that facilitation can involve coaching, mentoring and counselling as they are needed, the leader can be much more effective in drawing out more of the skills and talents of the people he or she is working with. Can you imagine how much more successful they would be if they always achieved or overachieved their anticipated outcomes of these meetings, through better facilitation.

Leadership, if it ever was, is no longer about creating a group of blind followers. It is about finding and nurturing the best in people – inside and beyond the business – to take the business in directions and at a speed that might seem beyond the capabilities of the leader alone but not beyond the team.

Being a leader in business today is no longer about 'hard' or 'soft' skills. It is about both skillsets in balance. The ability to read a balance sheet and to read a person is equally important. Bottom line results only come through the skills and commitment of the whole team. Just like a Premiership football manager, the leader needs to motivate a wide variety of already talented individuals so that the team is far greater than the sum of the individual players.

World-class facilitation will get you there and I know that all 12 attendees on Darren's course will go and achieve beyond their wildest dreams.

[15]**http://www.darrenrudkin.co.uk/**

Making better decisions

Decisions

One of the joys of growing a business is that you can delegate the easier decisions to others. The bigger the business grows, the more and more complex decisions you can delegate. The downside of this is that you are left with only the tougher decisions to make. Investment, disciplinary and dismissal and closing down unproductive areas of the business are just some of the areas where the buck is likely to stop with you as the Chief Executive.

So it is useful to have a process for making decisions. Not everyone does. We all know people who make decisions instantly but sometimes regret them later and people who keep on gathering more and more facts and opinions and seemingly never decide on anything.

There are three stages to making a decision. The first -- and most important -- is to frame the right question. Unless you know what you have to decide, you are unlikely to make a good decision.

Stage two is research and consultation. It is here that many people make mistakes, either by skimping or by over elaborating. Either extreme can have unexpected consequences. You could think of the decision as a chasm between two solid pieces of land – your starting point and your hoped-for destination. There is a drop between the two points which may be shallow or deep. The difference between the two points is the gap of knowledge and information that needs to be bridged whilst the drop represents the risk if the gap is not properly negotiated.

If you can bridge the chasm completely, the decision should probably have been made elsewhere and not have come to you. Your role as Chief Executive is to work with decisions where the bridge does not fully span the chasm -- that is, there are still unknowns – and where there is a deep drop if the remaining gap is not properly cleared – that is there is significant risk if the decision is not right.

Finally, there is a point at which you need to take a decision. The bigger the gap and the deeper the drop, the more risky the decision but potentially the more rewarding the result. Your competitors may be prepared to take bigger decisions than you and if they come off, they will take a lead. The big question is, do you continue as you are and trust in their decisions failing or take a positive leap of your own into a better future?

Only you can answer this for your company and, be sure, you will be judged on it by your shareholders, your board, your competitors and your customers.

There is a very important fourth stage to this process. Having made the decision, it must be acted upon and it must be monitored. For some decision makers, the hardest part of this process is in the first step towards its implementation and selling the decision to those who are affected by it.

If you have a clear understanding of how the business should perform when the decision is having a positive impact, then you will be able to notice when this is not the case and make the necessary changes, including reversing the decision if necessary, for the good of the business.

Remember, when you are faced with seemingly wall-to-wall difficult or intractable problems, that this is the result of your own personal success and represents the challenge that you sought. You owe it to yourself and to your team to make good decisions – decisions made with care, compassion and love.

Sometimes we can be our own worst enemy. When the company needs us to be at our best and most inventive, we get stuck and find ourselves unable to answer important questions facing us – questions that we think need answering. No matter how we try, the answer doesn't seem to really address the issue. There has, you think, to be a better answer.

At times like these, it is often worth considering if the question is what limits us – that it doesn't actually give us scope to find a good answer. What we need is not a better answer but a better question.

A better question is one that opens up the area of the problem to allow more scope for developing solutions. Rather than focusing in on the problem, a better question views the whole system. It is like going up in a helicopter and looking down on the problem area. You gain perspective and are able to see the pattern of cause and effect more easily. It allows for the possibility that what you are seeing is not the cause but the effect. For example, your sales team are not closing enough business. It would be easy to suppose that the sales team are at fault, but what if your marketing messages are attracting the wrong prospects or you are spending time trying to sell products that are no longer competitive?

By asking a better question, one that opens up the possibility of other causes, the business will benefit and so will you. It will be one less headache to contend with.

Intuition and Gut decisions

Somewhere inside achievers they have the ability to make quick and fast decisions. This decision comes from a well honed, well-oiled visceral computer or as it is often called 'inside our gut'

Scientists can explain this and it is very important to recognise that we have a huge ability to access information and make decisions, a process which is naturally within all of us. Everyone has it. Everyone has intuition within us. We generally believe that women have more intuition than men. I have heard my wife sum up somebody straight way and she is always right. Well I believe we all have it. It is not gender based.   Men, however, often talk themselves out of their first decision by using logic and often this leads to a decision that they realise later was wrong. How often do we say *'I wish I had listened to my gut feel, I knew that that person was wrong when I first met them'.*

If we change our belief about intuition and use it as an innate instrument that has built up over our life time, even perhaps before we were born, as soon as we face somebody or a situation, that intuition comes into play. It comes to us as a gut feel, as a response, which, if we hear it, is usually right. So to make better and quicker decisions, not to miss opportunities, we must listen and act and learn to appreciate our intuition. We use our intuition when we fall in love with someone at first sight. It is our intuition that tells us whether they are right or wrong. When we are employing people for a job, if we use our intuition as well as psychometric tests we are more likely to make the right decision.

I have run several group interviews. In the last one I became really aware of the power of my intuition. We split the groups into two lots of 10 and there were three of us interviewing. I wanted to put the 10 in order of merit within 2 minutes from the moment when the candidates had come into the room. We then spent the morning doing various tests. Half way through I suggested that we mark them again at the end of the meeting. We did this twice with two separate groups of 10. All three of us came up with same first, second and third from both lots of 10. We took on the three top candidates in both sections and they have turned out to be highly successful.

Exercise – *you are employing a finance director*

There are three people applying for the job; interview them as a group. After just two minutes of the interview, you and your colleagues all mark them individually one to ten. score of one being the candidate is unemployable and ten being outstanding. Then mark them again after one hour, and again at the conclusion of the interview.

You will be surprised to note that your intuition after just two minutes will find you the best candidate. This rarely changes over the period of the interview.

If you do this and you can do it in several instances, you can do it when you meet new friends –say at a dinner party. Just on your napkin, write down the very first number relating to your initial impression of them and see how it changes/differs at the end of an evening.

So think of your intuition as a computer within you that gives an intelligent response based on all millions of experiences you have had. The results will be accurate and the only thing that changes this is when you try to work out logically why this happens. Learn when you have not used your intuition and that way you will quickly accept the first response. You will save time, prevent mistakes and ensure that you succeed.

We all talk to ourselves and probably most conflicts come from the places within us that are discussing something, talking about something, arguing about something. This is happening all the time and we are making decisions all the time. This voice comes from a different place; this voice comes from the gut.

This voice is your intuition, your visceral computer. But unlike a computer, you can't turn it off.

Learn from it,
listen to it, *and* act on it. *It is always right!*

5. Leading a Company

"Great leaders...
motivate *large groups of individuals*
to **improve** *the human condition."*

John Kotter

Company versus team

For early stage companies, company leadership is the same as team leadership. There is only one team and the numbers of people involved are manageable. As companies grow, so they change from a simple team into a complex of teams and the bigger the company gets, the more that complexity begins to affect leadership. Companies are still about people first but there are many more considerations and it can be easy to forget the people with the other issues of strategy, brand and the day to day challenges of balancing growth with cash flow. Also, as the team grows, a company culture develops but not always in the ways you would like it to. Consultants frequently remark on how different companies actually are from the description they get from the top team on engagement. That can be a problem.

In this chapter, I have included a number of sections that describe the approach set out by Jim Collins in *Good to Great*, his 2001 book analysing companies that have successfully made the leap from good to truly great performance. I make no apology for this. The book is worth reading in its entirety and his approach fits well with mine.

The Right People

Most strategies focus on the goal and then look for the right people to achieve it. If the business were a bus, the destination would be on the front from the outset as people waited at the stops to join it. Collins finds that the companies who satisfied the criteria set by his research team approached the strategy from another angle. Instead of working out where to go first, the GTG companies tended to concentrate on getting the right people on the bus and in the right seats first *(and getting the wrong people off)* then figuring out where to drive it.

From a funding point of view, choosing the right people first seems like a high-risk strategy but the evidence from Collins seems to suggest that the companies who approach things in this way tend to find different *(and maybe better)* places to go.

The great companies in Collins' study also showed a difference in leadership style when compared with similar companies whose growth was lower over the same period. Many companies operated the *'genius with a thousand helpers'* approach, where one person *(or a small group)* is seen as THE leader and the rest of the members of the team were seen as followers. The *'great'* companies tended to operate as Level 5 Management teams *(see previous chapter)* where leadership runs deep and the loss of one charismatic leader would not jeopardise company performance.

You may be thinking that this approach demands too much from the business to be useful for you. Collins seems to recognise this, too and offers three practical ideas to help make it workable for your business.

The first is that when in doubt, don't hire but keep looking for the right person. You should limit growth based on ability to attract enough of the right people. Offering more money is not a guarantee of finding the right people but it does keep the right people in place, once you have found them.

The second is excellent advice, in my opinion. When you know you need to make a people change, act as soon as possible. But first make sure that they aren't just in the wrong seat.

Finally, he suggests,

> *You should put your* **best people** *on your* **biggest opportunities**, **not** *on your biggest problems...*

and if you sell off your problems, don't sell off your best people with them.

Once the team is formed, members should be encouraged to debate vigorously and then unify behind decisions. In the great companies there were plenty of different opinions but parochial and political interests were considered secondary to the best interests of the team and the business.

It is often said that people are your greatest asset; Collins insists that the RIGHT people are your biggest asset and it is worth taking the time to ensure that you have the best people in all roles.

One of the vital roles in a business is that of the Board. I frequently get asked, should we take on a Non-Executive Director (NED) and, if so, what role should a NED play? These are important questions. It seems that there is much confusion in the minds of some directors of SME companies about this. Since Cadbury redefined the roles and responsibilities of NEDs in larger businesses, their role has been to ensure that corporate governance is being maintained. They can be held personally liable if failures occur during their term of office.

As a result, people perceive the role of the NED in a non-corporate business as being legal and onerous, neither of which is true in practice. They are, however, capable of providing experience and skills to a growing business that might be hard to find elsewhere. So should an SME take on a NED? Almost certainly yes but they need to define the role and duration of the appointment in order to get the right person.

Whether the appointment is as a Chairman or in some other area of the business, if the intention is to reach the contacts and to benefit from the experience that a NED brings, the duration of the engagement should be fixed from the start, probably at one or two years. It can always be extended if that makes business sense. Make sure that there is a definition of their role and of the expectations of their performance and appraise them as you would any other senior team member against their Key Performance Indicators (KPIs). Write it all down and agree it in advance.

Do NEDs need to be 'friends or family'? Bringing friends or family into the business as NEDs can backfire. You will need to separate business from the friendship or other relationship. Either of you may have to tell the other something they don't want to hear in the interests of building a better business. Unless you are prepared for that to happen, either the friendship or the business or both may suffer.

In family businesses, or where the Directors all share significant history, the Non-Executive Chairman – in this case he or she must be independent - has a very specific role. He or she must make sure that Board Meetings happen and that the figures, along with Directors' monthly reports, are delivered and scrutinised. The Non-Executive Chairman needs to apply rigour to the management of the business.

Where corporate NEDs shoulder considerable risk and expect to get paid accordingly, SME based NEDs are much less prone to risk but their influence on the performance of a growing company can be the difference between nearly making it and substantial, sustainable success.

Make sure that both you and your chosen NED know exactly what you want to achieve. I'm a great believer in experience being a benefit in business. Why go through the pain of making mistakes when there is someone available who already knows what to do and can provide an answer and quickly add value? Experience gets you where you want to be more quickly. Well, mostly it does. There are two pitfalls that you need to avoid in order to use experience best.

The first is that the experience and knowledge must be transferred during the process. Wherever possible, make sure there is a mentoring relationship in place with one of your team so that next time a similar problem is encountered, there is someone in the team who can tackle it.

The second is that not everyone who offers experience also has the creativity to apply it properly to your business. They are valuable to you only if they are able to match their experience well to the problem at hand and supply a solution that will work for you. No two problems are alike and yours may differ from the experience you adviser has had. A good advisor will be able to adapt the solution to your needs or recognise that the solution is not the right one.

Adding an experienced person to your Board is often a good way to move the business forward. Whilst you may choose such a person for a specific role for which they have appropriate experience, adding someone who is able to apply creativity as well as experience provides you with a truly powerful resource.

My experience with our mastermind groups is that ten experienced people who are able to recognise and synthesise their very different experience and skills produce incredibly high quality results. Your Board can have the same creativity and energy with the right appointments.

*The **really good people** in business*
***never stop learning**
and **never stop listening**

As I've already said, having the right people 'on the bus' is crucial to the success of any business. So how is it that some businesses seem to hold on to their talented people and others simply do not?

Good people are hard to find and often expensive to recruit, so when you find the right people it makes sense to hang on to them. Talented people become an asset to the business and make it easier to find new customers or clients. Maybe they have a following of their own *(amongst staff as well as clients)* that would leave with them if they should leave you. They are a risk as well as an asset.

These key people choose to work for *(with)* you and can choose not to if they are not happy. It isn't about money, either, though paying too little may be a de-motivator, paying more money isn't usually a motivator.

So what factors create satisfaction? They are achievement, recognition, the work itself, responsibility, advancement and growth. My own experience bears this out. You need to create an environment in which people can thrive. Becoming a world-class employer is about creating a place where employee views are listened to and respected, where there is transparency in the decision making process and where bullying and unfair treatment of employees is not tolerated. If people feel safe and valued, they are more creative and innovative, adding to the value of the business for customers and shareholders alike.

You can easily recognise a productive workplace – it is the one where the people look as though they are enjoying being there.

Ever heard anyone say - "**I never ask my people to do anything that I couldn't do myself.**"? They've obviously never heard about leverage. Would you only use a crane to lift weights that you could lift yourself or load a lorry only with what you can carry on your back? Of course not – and it is the same with people.

Modern business is complex and involves finding and using a variety of skills that contribute to the success of the business. The chances of your being able to do every task competently yourself is low and deluding yourself that you can may be dangerous to the health of the business. If the only brain that matters in the business is yours, your business will be limited to what you know.

So how do you take the leap from being the single guiding light into a business of many specialists who together create something that is better than any one person could have produced, where the whole is greater than the sum of all the parts?

The first and significant step is to recognise that the change is happening and to embrace it. Fighting it simply produces tension and often results in your brighter people moving on. From spending much of your time in making decisions, meeting suppliers, selling to customers and whatever else day to day work looks like for you, you need to make a switch to setting direction, motivating people and providing the environment in which they can succeed. It is a whole new set of skills and you will need to learn them.

Setting direction is about knowing where the business is heading and what the results will be like when it gets there. It is not about deciding how each team member will get there. Motivated people will provide their own solutions to that particular problem and they may just be better, more elegant and more profitable than yours. Keeping people motivated and moving in the same direction is your most important role as a leader. Some of your key people will be working in areas where you have experience and knowledge and some will not. Regardless of which area they fall into, your role is to get the best out of them. It is, perhaps, easier to do that with people who do jobs you don't know inside out because you have to judge their performance objectively. With practice you can do the same for all.

Getting the best out of your people requires an ability to coach them. Coaching generally involves a structured process such as that employed by the **G R O W** model championed by Sir John Whitmore[16] and is aimed at short to medium term performance improvements. There will be a number of steps through which problems can be explored and solutions developed. **GROW**, for example, identifies the **G**oals to be achieved, the current **R**eality of the situation, explores **O**pportunities to overcome current problems or delays and comes up with an action plan (**W**hat's next in **GROW** model terms). Once solutions have been agreed, they can be monitored using the same process.

Coaching elicits a wide range of reactions amongst business people. Some can see no place for it in business - it is too 'touchy feely' and 'real' managers just get on with it, do their jobs and "don't need all that stuff". Others ignore the 'new age' connotations of coaching and recognise that good sportspeople become great sportspeople with the right coaching and that good businesspeople also need help to become great. Coaching is as much about having the right attitude as it is about training.

[16]**Coaching For Performance: Growing People, Performance and Purpose**
(Nicholas Brealey Publishing 2002

If you are already a good listener – to verbal and non-verbal communication – the chances are that you already coach people and help them. The key to applying coaching across your business is to do it in a structured fashion and to do it consistently. There are many techniques that will help you to refine your coaching skills. Open questioning encourages the person being coached to seek their own answers and Neuro Linguistic Programming *(NLP)* or Psychology courses can help you with picking up on the often underlying issues that people cannot or will not volunteer to you.

The better you get at coaching, the more you'll feel comfortable in asking people to perform way beyond your own capabilities and limitations. It is all about leverage. Small efforts can produce major effects.

What has given me most pleasure over my 40-plus years as a leader has been finding for people in my companies, the position that is right for them. I have promoted people from warehouse jobs into management who subsequently went on to be general managers. To me, motivating people is about putting them into jobs that they enjoy and love. It makes people happier and more successful. Believe me, the two things go together.

A business that is full of happy and motivated people is more likely to succeed than one that is not. It also spills over into other aspects of their lives. Happy people generally have happier families, too.

In *The Human Side of the Enterprise*[17] , Douglas McGregor, suggested that there are two approaches to motivating a workforce called Theory X and Theory Y. Theory X assumes that employees are inherently lazy and will avoid work if they can whilst Theory Y assumes that employees may be ambitious, self- motivated and ready to take on greater responsibility. You may guess which theory I tend to support. The important word in Theory Y is 'may'. Not everyone is interested in promotion and advancement. However, I do believe that whoever they are and whatever they do, they want to a good job and should be encouraged and enabled to do so. I would find a Theory X workplace stifling and would probably not thrive there – that may be true of employees in such an environment, too.

This may seem unusual, but I believe that you should love your employees unconditionally. You should be there to support them and to help them succeed, both for themselves and for the company. When you employ someone, you don't

---

[17]**https://www.mcgraw-hill.co.uk/html/0071462228.html**

just get the part of them that does the job for you for 35 or so hours a week – you get the whole person and they deserve to be considered and supported when decisions are made. They are not counters to be moved around a game board, they are human beings.

Sometimes, loving someone means that you have to make difficult decisions. They might not be good at their job and, despite your efforts to help and support them, you may need to part company with them. Even at this time, it can be done with love and concern. If things have come to head in this way, very often the employee in question also feels that their performance is not good enough and that they need to make a change. It is better to part company as friends than to do so with rancour and bad feeling on both sides.

If you recognise that you might be a Theory X type of leader *(there are plenty of resources and even tests online to help you work this out)* and you are not getting the results that you need from your business, give your people the benefit of the doubt and some solid support and just see what might happen.

It might just make you happier, too.

Culture

Achievers create a spirituality which surrounds them and drives them and takes them to places which have meaning. It is hard to know what spirituality is or to describe it. Many people think that spirituality equals religion or religious belief. We want to think that religious people have spirituality, but I do believe many non-religious people have spirituality, have powerful beliefs, are caring and compassionate and they create an aura, an environment around them that can perhaps be called a culture. They create a state that people will follow. Above all they create love for their fellow man.

The interesting thing about spirituality is that you can't measure it in Key Performance Indicators and you can't do a psychometric test to see whether an organisation has a heart or a soul. For me this very important element of organisation of businesses that create wealth or success because they have bundles of spirituality within their people. The feeling that anyone gets when they go into this type of organisation would be one where the environment exudes peace or fun and where the people are smiling and happy; where politically in fighting is unacceptable; where creativity is the core of what people are doing and where the heart in the company exudes love, caring and that everyone in it just enjoys coming to that place. I deliberately didn't say 'coming to work' but coming to have pleasure all the time.

Achievers in business today and in the future will need to keep and attract talented people. That will only happen by creating spirituality within the business that people find a nourishing place to go to. Money will not be the main driver but a happy place where people feel valued for the achievements that they make.

Clearly to create a spiritually based company in business, the attitude and actions of the leaders are vital. An interesting company which has been winning many awards for their business and as one of the top companies to work for is a food manufacturing company. Once this company didn't care about their people and was managed by the leader who was a control freak, who demanded action, didn't believe in teamwork. The company didn't have a smiling feeling. The workers were paid very little to work on the factory floor and were not happy at all. It is very interesting that this same person, with some mentoring was able to bring out his natural values. A single change for him was when I suggested he demonstrate vulnerability to his people rather than appearing to know it all. He would admit that maybe he had made a mistake or maybe someone else knew better than him. When he did it, that one single thing changed the attitude the whole way down the line. That one single thing changed the spirituality within the business and success on the bottom line at the same time. It was very interesting to observe the changes that took place within the whole organisation.

The leader found it was much easier for him to get support by sharing rather than telling. He found other people were coming up with ideas not relying on him all the time. He found things that were important to the profitability of the business like wastage suddenly disappeared because people cared about what they were doing. He found that staff turnover on the factory level suddenly stopped because people actually enjoyed working there even though it was a low salary and they would not leave just for a higher salary because their colleagues were happier and they become friends. The whole environment changed from what we started with. People were getting recognised for the work they did, even though they might not get a bonus for it, there was maybe a written note or praise given by the leader. That went through the whole leadership team.

Nature will always try to fill a vacuum and employees will always try to fill a communications vacuum. The result is what is known as the grapevine and it is at its most active and effective in a company that chooses not to communicate with its employees.

Let me begin by stressing that you can't control what your employees (including fellow directors) think and say. What you can do is to provide them with the company's view on topics that are otherwise likely to become the subject of lurid speculation. That just may reduce or remove the more extreme rumours that would otherwise circulate.

There is a point of view that suggests that employees are not assets of the business but simply volunteers who can, and often do, take their services elsewhere. We cannot prevent that, but we can make it less likely by making sure that employees feel involved in the business. There are many ways to do this.

Some smaller businesses have a weekly get-together where communication can take place. It is usually a two-way process with the Chief Executive and his team getting as much information as they give. The effect in terms of information sharing and morale is often crucial to business development. The difficult trick to perfect is to achieve this same two-way communication as the company grows and, maybe, operates from multiple sites. Whilst the top team still have to be visible, involving visits to all parts of the business on a regular basis, any communications strategy that depends on this alone is doomed to failure - and an active grapevine.

Cascading announcements may take care of the communication from the Board downwards but are poor at bringing information back to the centre. There are too many filters in the process and that may also affect the quality of the delivery of news from the Board as well. Intranets were a solution that began to emerge in the last decade of the 20th century though most were still one way mechanisms and some were little more than online phone directories and operations manuals. For a 21st century solution, we have to look at tools like MySpace, Facebook, Twitter and YouTube.

The main feature of those sites is the informality of the way information is shared. In Facebook, anyone can contribute their profile and their thoughts. Debates begin to develop that produce results. YouTube and MySpace both cater for other forms of communication than the written word. Video over the internet allows your message to be shared over a widely dispersed group of people who can watch when they want to *(and as often as they need to)*.

There are business networking sites *(Ecademy, Linkedin, and Xing)* and many business blogs where you can learn how best to use the many communications options that now exist. For most businesses, the free and easy approach of

Selecting the right strategy

Having got the right people in the right seats on the bus and confronted the brutal facts, whilst remaining confident of success, this is the crucial process for deciding 'what' the destination for the business will be.

Jim Collins quotes Isiah Berlin about hedgehogs and foxes. "Whilst the fox knows many things, the hedgehog knows one big thing". Great companies, Collins and his research team found, were mostly hedgehogs. They had come to the realisation that they had a simple and clear purpose and that brought them great results.

So it may be useful to know how to be a hedgehog. Collins proposes that finding your 'Hedgehog Concept' consists of understanding the answer to three questions represented as three circles. Finding an answer that is at the intersection of all three is most powerful.

The first question is deceptively simple but gets more difficult to answer each time you ask it. *What can you be the best in the world at?* This is not what you are merely good at and it may not be your current core competence. Being the best in the world at what you do demands serious thought and may result in changing track completely. For Kimberly Clark, it meant becoming the best in the world at developing consumer products using paper rather than manufacturing. To make that change, they sold all of their paper mills.

The second question is about ensuring that there is a compass to steer by. *What drives your economic engine?* The answer should preferably be a single measure that encapsulates your Hedgehog quest. For Kimberly Clark it became profit per consumer brand, for Gillette, profit per customer and for Walgreens *(a convenience drugstore group in the USA)* profit per customer visit. For each of them, if the measurement improved, the company grew profitably. The right measure may take time to discover but when it has been, it is something that everyone in the business will be able to understand and support.

Finally, the third circle asks *what are you deeply passionate about?* Finding something to do and then motivating people to be passionate about it will not be good enough to make a great company. The company has to do those things its people can get passionate about and the motivation and enthusiasm will happen.

Getting from Good to Great may be the application of simple principles but no one said that it would be easy to apply them. It takes time to find the right starting point and more time to refine the concept and, once found, it needs determination and discipline to keep to it.

One approach that Collins suggests is 'The Council'. The Council is a group of people from within the business who are charged with finding and driving the Hedgehog Concept. Being part of Collins' Good to Great approach, the Council naturally needs the right people on the bus and they need not be Board members or senior executives – ideally representation from all levels should be sought. The Council follows an iterative process always bearing in mind the three circles – they ask questions and then have dialogue and debate around them. They will reach executive decisions – not always a consensus – and run autopsies and analysis of their effectiveness, confronting brutal facts as always. That will inevitably lead to more *(and better)* questions.

Greatness is only achieved by doing the right things consistently. That takes understanding across the business and a truly disciplined approach.

Branding is an exercise that starts and ends with the leader. There may be elements of it that belong in the marketing department, including logo design, but the major elements of it are central to how the company will be seen both inside and outside the business.

We need to ask ourselves `*what do we stand for, what do we do and how does that meet the audience's needs?'* in order to find something compelling, resonant and emotionally true from which to build a credible, relevant, sustainable, different promise". They are very much 'Hedgehog' questions.

Brand is about the very core of the business. It consists of a number of factors including purpose, vision, essence, beliefs, behaviours and core messages – as well as compelling and consistent iconography. It is the key to opening up the business to understanding by those who will engage with it. These people might include customers, partners, suppliers and, for a membership organisation, members. Often these groups of people are referred to as your stakeholders.

Your brand can become shorthand for the values and promises you deliver in the marketplace. It is important to ensure that this shorthand is consistent with the values and promises that you want it to deliver. A skewed brand can become a liability but a clear and congruent brand is an asset that can be valued on the balance sheet – it has a real value.

If the brand is articulated clearly and communicated widely, it is easier for employees to work within it and to give customers and other stakeholders the right experience when dealing with the business. It ensures understanding and consistency and helps in the development of a culture within the business.

Of course, it should go without saying that, once articulated, everyone is an ambassador for the brand. That includes the Leader – indeed the Leader should be leading in this area above all others.

I have seen many businesses struggle, over the years, after changing their 'brand' – often with just a new logo and strapline – but not changing the underlying culture to live up to the new image. Worse, some make promises about customer experiences that they are simply not geared up to deliver. Would you put your reputation at risk in that way?

Brand, as I hope I have demonstrated, begins and ends in the Chief Executive's office. If you are uncertain how a new proposition or brand can be delivered, imagine how it will be for your team and for your customers.

You need the right brand but it has to be implemented in the right way to provide you with the full benefit.

I was once told the story of two business leaders who were sitting on a bench looking into the night sky. *"Which is the nearest,"* asked one, *"the moon or Nebraska?"* *"Simple,"* replied the other, *"The moon, of course, I can't see Nebraska,"*

"'The President of the United States,' wrote Henry Adams, the most brilliant of American historians, *'resembles the commander of a ship at sea. He must have a helm to grasp, a course to steer, a port to seek.'* The Constitution awards presidents the helm, but creative presidents must possess and communicate the direction in which they propose to take the country. The port they seek is what the first President Bush dismissively called *'the vision thing."* - State of the 'Vision Thing' by Arthur M. Schlesinger Jr, (Los Angeles Times 21/1/04)*[18]

The 'Vision Thing' is important for leaders and for those who they employ, too. If we are to create something that has never existed before, we first need to be able to 'see' it in our mind before attempting to make it real. Without that step, we may fail to believe in the project or product simply because we can't see it.

The process of visioning may involve creating mental models, drawings, narratives, role-plays and physical models of the thing we wish to create. The better the

[18] http://articles.latimes.com/2004/jan/21/opinion/oe-schlesinger21

clarity of the vision the more likely it is that all in the process can 'see' the same thing and will endeavour to make it happen.

The American President best remembered for his clarity of vision and his exemplary communication of it to a whole nation was John F Kennedy who in May 1961 told the US Congress, *"I believe that this nation should commit itself to achieving the goal, before this decade is out, of landing a man on the moon and returning him safely to the earth."* In the full speech is clear that he understood how daunting that goal would be, however, he convinced the American people that it could be done and, in July 1969, they saw it achieved.

George Bush, Sr. may have disparaged the 'Vision Thing' but for Chief Executives it is a crucial tool for innovation and achievement.

"At last the Dodo said, 'everybody has won, and all must have prizes.'" *- Alice in Wonderland.*

Are business awards worth the effort of entering? Can they really be a benefit to your business? The answer to both questions can be yes but only if you know why you have entered and have clear expectations from the awards process. If you win or get a positive mention it can be a huge boost to internal morale amongst your team. Publicising the award can also positively affect potential clients' view of you as a business.

Choosing the right awards scheme can also be important. They vary widely in their approach and their rigour. Some schemes don't even visit or talk with the entrants, judging them purely on the submission they make whilst others, like the Best Companies to Work For survey, run by Best Companies Limited and published in the Sunday Times, go much further than that.

The best people to judge who are the best companies to work for are the employees and, fittingly, Best Companies, operate an employee survey that measures responses on leadership, managers, personal growth, wellbeing, the team, impact on society, and how employees feel about the company and its pay and benefits. The judges also visit many companies. The result is an Awards scheme that matters to the company and to its employees and trading partners.

All entrants get feedback on their entry, too – a valuable benefit in its own right. Imagine however how the employees and customers of W.L Gore, winners of the Overall Best Company award again in 2007, must feel. Or how anyone associated with P3, the social inclusion charity, is lifted by their rise to become the best SME to work for in 2007 from 26th in 2006. I dare say that there is a feeling of hard work rewarded. The Awards probably brought focus to the organisation and will have a longer term effect on their performance.

Awards are positive but only if you approach them with the right attitude and are prepared to learn from early setbacks, putting the work in to ensure a better performance next time.

Rather like any feedback in business, it is only of use if you listen, learn and adapt.

Maintaining Momentum

How does technology play its part in moving from Good to Great in Business? Jim Collins and his team asked themselves whether dominance in a technology could lead a company to make the transition from Good to Great. The experience of their research says that technology is not a major factor in making the transition possible but that technology can improve and accelerate the transition from Good to Great once it is underway. Other factors lead that process and we have already talked about most of them.

Collins and his team found that technology-led companies were still governed by the three circles of the Hedgehog Principle. My own observations confirm this. Many technology-led companies have the passion that is needed to succeed, fewer have the ability to be the best in the world at what they do but only a very few have the economic engine that is needed to make the transition. Too many technology companies are built on the mistaken belief that having a solution is enough. Unless enough people are asking the question to which your company has the solution and it is obvious to them where to get that solution at a price they are prepared to pay, there will not be a big enough market to make it a great solution and a great company.

So the advice with regards to technology is to put the basics in place first -

- **find Level 5 leadership**
- **have the right people on the bus**
- **confront the brutal facts**
- **work out their hedgehog principle - all three circles**
- **develop the discipline to move forward towards take off**

You can then find and implement the technology that supports these processes.

For the good to great businesses, technology was a late arrival in the process of transition, but when it came, it often made a profound difference to the speed of transition and to the eventual market position of the business. Collins comments that *"you could have taken the exact same leading-edge technologies pioneered at good to great companies and handed them to their direct comparisons for free, and the comparisons would have failed to produce anywhere near the same results".*

Technology is important in the right place but according to Collins' findings, that place is as an accelerator of momentum and not as a creator of it.

If the book Good to Great has its own 'Hedgehog Principle' – that is if it 'knows one big thing' – then it would be, for me, the idea of the flywheel. For what the flywheel tells us is that greatness comes from consistently building momentum within the business and not from quick fix initiatives and attempts to change the whole business in one big push.

If you imagine a huge and heavy wheel that requires huge effort even to make it move, and then consider the effects of consistently pushing it in one direction what may be a very long time, you may begin to see that, once moving, each push can add progressively more momentum to the movement of the wheel. The wheel accelerates. No one push on the flywheel allows it to reach 'escape' velocity but many pushes over a period of time, each in the same direction, will do so, providing that no one stops the momentum by trying to move it in another direction.

What this metaphor, at the heart of the book, tells us is that great companies may seem like an overnight success, but the effort predates the transition to greatness by many years. Moving a business forward in a single direction requires certainty and consistency, hence the need to be sure about the right direction in which to push. This is what led to the realisation that who is on the bus is more important than where it is going at the start and that the three circles of the hedgehog principle, once understood, give a business the right direction.

The opposite effect to the flywheel is that of the doom loop. The research into comparison companies showed that some companies fail because they keep changing direction not allowing momentum to take hold. Typically such businesses had lots of 'initiatives' - many with names and internal promotional material, made acquisitions that were intended to speed breakthrough to greatness but actually took the company off track. New leaders who changed the direction of travel of companies also ensured that no momentum was being built or, worse, that momentum that had been built was lost. In these companies, the doom loop applied and the company often spiralled downwards leading to increasingly desperate initiatives and further downward spirals.

Companies that managed to achieve a sustainable transition had, according to Collins, "a predictable pattern of build up and breakthrough". It took a lot of effort to get the change moving but less effort once the flywheel was turning. People inside the business were often unaware of the magnitude of the transition that was happening and there was no internal naming/branding of initiatives, just a steady accumulation of activity that leads to breakthrough.

I would recommend reading Good to Great for yourself and then applying the principles to your own circumstances. There are many questions to ask about people, direction, discipline and the hedgehog principle for your business.

But if you ask only one question of your business, make it - are you turning the flywheel or facing the doom loop?

If it is the flywheel – I congratulate you.

If the doom loop – maybe it is time for a hard look at the business and to face some brutal facts. All may not be lost but it is time to take action.

Getting from good to great is a matter of finding the right formula for the business. The real effort is in staying great. That is a real a team effort with proper *(Level 5)* leadership and a simple *(Hedgehog)* concept. But temptations come along and businesses seem to be programmed to pursue opportunities even when they are not exactly what they should be doing. How can this 'creep' into non-Hedgehog areas be resisted?

The business needs to provide freedom and responsibility within a framework that can be understood and applied. Collins proposes that take off from good to great comes from the process of disciplined people, applying disciplined thought and leading to disciplined action.

All this talk of discipline caused Collins to doubt whether this section was rightly in the GTG formula. After all, there were many examples of charismatic leaders acting in a tyrannical way to impose discipline on their business – and the results did, in many cases, respond positively to that. However, the team decided that it was a culture of discipline that was what made companies move from good to great and stay there, not a tyrant. The difference is that the tyrant needs to be there for growth and performance to happen whereas a culture ensures growth and performance happen independent of leadership.

Fanatical adherence to the Hedgehog Concept along with the belief that *"we WILL find a way"* often leads directly to great performance. When distractions, however apparently lucrative, appear, the business will apply a simple test - anything that does not fit, we will not do – and the people within the business will understand why some opportunities are turned down.

Collins also proposes, at an individual as well as corporate level, creating the 'stop doing' list on the grounds that if it doesn't fit - stop doing it. Kimberley Clark as they moved from paper production to consumer products stopped attending Paper Industry Steering groups. Collins also proposes a change to the purpose of budgets. Budgeting, he suggests, is not to decide how much money goes to each area or project but rather to decide what is fully funded and what is not funded at all.

Throughout the book, the sections refer back to each other. The whole structure of Collins approach to greatness in businesses is co dependent. To follow the Hedgehog Concept with the necessary systematic discipline can only happen if the right people are on the bus. Those people need to be passionate, self-leading, disciplined, focused, skilled and knowledgeable.

Taking over at a company, as opposed to building one from formation, can be a difficult and sensitive task. So it is with political leadership. In 2007, as Tony Blair stepped down as the UK's ultimate Chief Executive and Gordon Brown took over, I began thinking about some of the issues involved in taking on the role of Chief Executive in a new business, or, as was the case with Brown, stepping up from another senior role in the same business.

A change of Chief Executive is an important transition for any business and it often takes place in a blaze of publicity. Some businesses will merit front page news whilst many others will appear in the business pages. If the business is listed on the Stock Exchange, the share price may be affected and in private companies, both shareholders and employees will be wary of any change which may affect their long term self interest.

It is tempting to make the big gesture - to make big changes in the first few days. A change of Board structure, maybe, or a change in the direction of the company but is it, in Brown's favourite word, prudent?

As a new hire at Chief Executive level, it is almost certainly better to take some time to assimilate the mountain of information and briefing that your senior team

– and all of the other team members – will provide you. You may be fortunate and have a trusted non executive team who can advise you on where to place your efforts initially but, even in the world of business, you have to beware of politics.

You can't wait too long, however, before you do something. If you do nothing for too long, there will be suggestions that you aren't decisive enough for the role. Perhaps what you need is a decision or decisions that appear to change something whilst giving you time to understand the effects of changes that really will change things – you hope for the better.

Of course, as a senior member of the team, you may be expected to know much more about the business already. The truth may, however, be different. You will understand the part of the business in which you were the key player but there may be areas that you have not been closely involved with. You may not know all of the decisions and policy directions that the previous Chief Executive had put in place. It is not unknown for a departing Chief Executive to leave behind a poisoned chalice. The temptation to reverse some policies and to change around the people and roles in the business is strong but may not always result in a better business. Your elevation within the business will also change your relationship with some people, not always for the better, another reason to spend some time assessing the effect of changes before you commit to them.

Gordon Brown's first weeks and months were examined in more detail and more publicly that any Chief Executive and it was an interesting process to follow and to learn from. He showed in his early approach to Sir Paddy Ashdown that he wanted to involve more people in the process of Government.

It may be that the most lasting impressions of his transition will be the way in which he was blown off course by events – donations to party funds, data losses at HMRC, MPs expenses and the wars in Iraq and Afghanistan – and his less than secure handling of them. Comparisons to his predecessor have already been made and they are not flattering to Brown. Maybe there was a poisoned chalice?

You've worked hard to get here. There have been times when it was impossible to relax for a moment as the business struggled for its survival in a competitive world. Then success arrived. You've begun to see the orders arriving and the profits building. This is what you've strived for all along, through all the years of penny pinching and close monitoring of every aspect of the business. **You can relax – can't you?**

Unfortunately, when success arrives is exactly the time not to relax. Success is not a constant and it will only continue if you work at it. It is easy, and very tempting, to get complacent at this stage of a business' life but it would be a bad mistake to do so. Any decision to increase expenditure and any temptation to ease off on the monitoring of the company's numbers carries a risk. Your competitors are not easing off. Neither should you.

I enjoy the game of cricket. In 2007, I watched with amazement as the seemingly invincible Australian one-day side slumped into a run of five straight defeats by England and New Zealand that, earlier in the season seemed unimaginable. If they eased back, it wasn't by much but it made a crucial difference. Their preparation for the Cricket World Cup was, as a result, tougher and more rigorous than it might otherwise have been.

The same inexplicable slump can overtake businesses when they, too, are at the top of their game. They may ease off, give less attention to the detailed numbers of the business and meet less often. Problems often surface first in the numbers. Sales may stop growing because of competitive activity, profitability may be eroded by materials price increases or salespeople give more discount than usual – all will be revealed in the numbers. Selling more of a product or service which is inherently profitable is a good thing, but what if it is no longer profitable and makes a small loss instead. The more units you sell before someone spots the problem, the more you will lose. Suddenly success is a bad thing.

Making sure you stay successful is about continuing to do the right things right. Every member of the Board is responsible for maintaining the winning position. Board meetings must be held regularly – every month at least – and the financial position must be monitored continuously.

Whose job is it to ensure all of this happens? The CEO, of course *(with the support of his Non-Executive Chairman if he has one)*. Snatching defeat from the jaws of victory is not part of his job description. Ensuring that everyone remains focused on further success clearly is.

I went to hear Jim Collins speak recently. He was every bit the excellent researcher and writer I expected him to be. What I didn't expect was how good a presenter he is, too. If you get the opportunity to see him live, take it. Otherwise, take a look at his website www.jimcollins.com which has plenty of resources that Chief Executives should find useful.

His current area of research is best described as 'great to good' – in other words what causes great companies to lose their edge. When things go wrong we often look for the point where they went wrong. We often miss the real point as we don't look back far enough. Collins contends that the triggering event is often several years in the past. It may be any form of change which can obscure the focus and cause the flywheel to slow – a new Chief Executive, a merger or acquisition or a change of environment (the new headquarters building for example). Companies can't stay complacent or begin to believe in their long-term greatness. They have to work at keeping great every day and in every interaction with their staff, their suppliers and, of course, their customers.

> ## "Keep in mind that neither success nor failure is ever final."
>
> **Roger Ward Babson**

As I have written here, the moment of success is the moment of most vulnerability. Be vigilant and keep focus, otherwise your success may begin to erode. Achieving greatness takes work and vision. Remaining great takes all of that plus an ability as Collins puts it to face up to 'the Brutal Facts' and lead the company to ever better performance.

Good and Bad Goals

Before he researched and wrote Good to Great, Jim Collins was involved in a six-year project at Stanford Business School which resulted in his co-authoring, with Jerry I. Porras, a book called Built to Last . The project examined "what was needed to start and build an enduring great company from the ground up".

At the outset of the Good to Great project, the team had to decide what role the Built to Last findings would play in the new project. It was decided, after much debate, to ignore them and begin the new project from a clean set of data. After the findings were clear, an exercise was undertaken to relate the findings of the Good to Great project with that of Built to Last, on the understanding that maintaining a great company would probably need elements of the latter as well as the former.

Collins now sees Good to Great as a 'prequel' to Built to Last and expresses the formula for enduring success as –

Established company or start-up + Good to Great concepts

= **Sustained great Results**

Sustained great Results + Built to Last concepts = **Enduring Great Company.**

Built to Last produced **four** key ideas –

1 **Clock Building, not Time Telling** – *"build an organisation that can endure and adapt through multiple generations of leaders and multiple product life cycles".*

2 **Genius of and.** *"Figure out how to have A and B rather than A or B"*

3 **Core Ideology.** *Importance of core values and core purpose in guiding decision and inspiring people over the long term.*

4 **Preserve the core/stimulate progress.** *"Preserve the core ideology as an anchor point whilst stimulating change, improvement, innovation and renewal in everything else".*

A part of the fourth idea is the belief that setting and achieving **BHAGs** *(Big Hairy Audacious Goals)* is important. Whilst Built to Last raised the idea of BHAGs, it was Good to Great, notes Collins, that distinguished between good and bad BHAGs. After all, even the comparison companies who didn't achieve greatness set them – in fact, charismatic leaders consistently set BHAGs. The difference is in the Hedgehog concept. BHAGs that fit into the space where all three elements of the Hedgehog concept intersect – passion, best in the world and driving the economic engine – are the most congruent goals a company can pursue.

So Good to Great added value to Built to Last in a way that gives a framework for making a company great and making that greatness endure.

I'll leave the last word on this to Jim Collins himself –

"To create an **enduring great company** *requires* **all the key concepts** *from both studies, tied together and* **applied consistently** *over time. Furthermore, if you ever stop doing any of the key ideas, your organisation will inevitably slide backward toward mediocrity"*

Jim Collins

6. Energy, Fitness and Wellbeing

"**Take care of your body**.
*It's the **only** place*
you have to live."

Jim Rohn

Business leaders are not immune from illness, nor are they immortal. To think otherwise would be to deny the obvious and to ignore the facts might be negligent in the extreme. Acting in denial of those facts might put the business at risk. That is not to suggest that it is not important for a leader to look after their health and fitness. That is a crucial element in being able to lead others. To try to do that when unable to look after your own welfare is likely to result in failure

Leaders need physical power and stamina and a positive mental attitude in order to be able to cope with the pressures of leadership. Our power is created by the energy we produce. The type of energy we produce and the direction in which we use it affects our ability to achieve and the time it takes us to achieve. When it turns to negative energy we will see how quickly it will take us to fail. Energy is our life force and we are responsible for feeding the furnace.

- *We provide the raw materials through food and drink,*
- *We develop its potential and efficiency through exercise and lifestyle*
- *We manage how it is applied through our thoughts, beliefs and actions.*

In this chapter, I want to look at all three of these elements, especially the area of mental attitude, which, I believe controls pretty much everything else. I also want to talk about the myth that we decline in our abilities as we get older. It is a dangerous myth and one that consigns able people to the scrapheap. To do this, I will also share some of my more recent journey and, in particular, how I am reversing my ageing process.

Mental Attitude

If energy is our life force and if our energy is controlled by our mind, if what we think is reality, we can use our mind to change, to develop or to reduce the energy we need and control the processes that ensure the energy we create is used to help us achieve.

The energy we use **helps** *us to* **develop** *the* **personality,** *the culture and the values that are* **important** *to us*

We can always be in control of our thoughts, however outside influences affect and often derail those thoughts and we need processes that can keep them in the direction that we want to go. If thoughts, conscious, subconscious or unconscious, manage and direct our energy then what are the tools and processes that we can use to ensure that they work for us and not against us.

Fitness – brain to body

Positive energy in all parts of your mind and body keeps you alive, keeps your wisdom intact and allows you to achieve goals in every part of your life. Staying fit inside your brain allows you to stay fit outside your brain. Always be ready to learn at whatever age. Continue to believe! Remember energy is mental, physical, emotional and spiritual. All parts need to be firing on all cylinders and this will only happen through the actions and beliefs that are always projected in a positive way.

When you are inspired by your purpose, or by a compelling project, your mind can overcome perceived limitations and your awareness expands in every direction. You find yourself in different dimension – a place where your achievements can multiply. As your inspiration grows, you awaken abilities, faculties and talents that you may not have suspected were there. You are able to be much more than you imagine you could be. Your mind can frequently exceed your expectations if you give it the chance to do so. You need a direction and a belief and the rest can follow.

The *quality of* your **life** *is determined by the* **quality of** *your* **thoughts**

There are no mistakes, only lessons. See setbacks as opportunities for personal expansion and spiritual growth.

Strategies

There are many strategies that we use to develop our thought processes and thus create our achievements. Perhaps the whole of this book goes some way to develop these strategies. Let's develop some of them now.

While reading these, clearly understand that these are strategies to develop your thoughts and your thought processes which create the direction, the speed and the power of your actions.

The first strategy that many people use is meditation. This is time put aside specifically to clear the mind of clutter and allow it to focus, to develop the thoughts that matter; a cleansing which takes away obstacles and leaves the profound. In the same way some people will use prayer. Prayer also gives the opportunity to clear the mind through focusing on a set of religious beliefs. Using music or song and chant can help the process, help to focus and to order your energy to work to the good.

I believe successful achievers find energy through prayer and meditation. Sometimes I feel that I am not meditating but lying there thinking about positive things. It doesn't matter about doing it right, just setting the time aside for thought and renewal is enough. What it does for me and maybe other successful achievers is that it cleanses the mind. So by an automatic hypnotic action you are turning negative feelings into positive feelings and thoughts. First you get a calm, relaxed state, and then you get positive thoughts. With those you can go about your daily work with real positive energy which enables you to achieve things you didn't think were possible. We certainly couldn't do them if we carried the negative thoughts around with us as we moved around.

When I work with CEOs, I see many of them arriving at work with their head down, with no energy having woken up at 4.00am in the morning thinking about all the bad things and not having transferred them over to the good things. If the leader is downbeat, that will affect all of the people around them. If you can avoid negative energy, that is obviously the best approach, but if you can't, it is better to act 'as if' you are positive and have the energy. In that way you may turn the negative energy into positive energy and, at least, transfer positive energy to everybody they meet that day. That works for me.

Arrive and remember to smile. However bad things are, remember to be positive and it is much easier to do that if you start with positive thoughts in your head. We forget that 99% of our life is positive and it only becomes negative if we let it become that way.

Self Talk

Another strategy that we all use, and in similar ways, is self-talk. Different voices in our head talk to each other and talk to us. We are doing this all the time and often conflict is created in our own mind by the different voices disagreeing with each other

A recent example of this for me was when my business was taking a turn for the worse in that, for the second time, one of my business partners decided that they were in the wrong place and wanted to move on. This created a litigious and unhealthy environment and a place where I felt myself moving into depression, considerably lacking in self esteem and belief in my own ability and the constant negative thought that as I was getting older I was losing my ability to create. As these negative thoughts moved up into my mind, I moved into depression, lacked energy and had little desire to achieve. The turn-round when it came was not luck. I remember clearly the point where I decided that I had to change the whole energy that I was giving out and wanted a positive mantra.

I made the decision in my mind to make that change and I still have the phrase 'Walk, tall, believe in what you have created, stop crying into your beard and stand up for your beliefs and values'. I listened to this self talk, took action on it and physically walked taller, used words that were more positive and changed completely the unhealthy environment that I had negatively created. Suddenly there was a new energy from the people who worked around me. The business which had stalled in one year was increased by over 100%. Colleagues who were barely supporting me suddenly became great advocates not only of our business processes but also of me personally. My self esteem was regained and it is a piece of learning I shall never forget.

I went through this process called voice dialogue understanding the voices within us. We all talk to ourselves but we sometimes don't realise the different voices that cause conflict in our heads. I recall when going through this process an issue that was causing me stress, whether to sell the business or not? One voice said 'if you sell the business you will have lots of money, no pension problem, lots of holidays etc.' Then another voice, reflecting my doubts, suggested 'sell the business and you will die. If you sell the business, what are you going to do and use your brain for?' I had never understood so clearly all these conflicting voices until I had the clarity that voice dialogue brought me. Therefore, since I had no wish to die, I was clearly able to decline the offer of sale.

So let's start to believe that the power of positive thought and self-talk will take you to places that you never believed that you could achieve, that you never expected to get to.

There are other things that can help you to bring your mind to focus on the positive. Firstly there is the creation of an environment that gives a focus on a more physical or more feeling place that allows your mind to focus and be positive. You will choose your own environment. It might be through physical exercise, yoga, painting, listening to music or by visiting art galleries. They will be activities and/or places that allow creativity to emerge and allow pictures or visions of your future whether short or long term.

Create an environment where wellness is important, where the food you eat creates the person that you want to be, creates the fitness of mind, creates a place where energy can prevail and illness can be avoided. Develop a place where you develop sports and hobbies where you can work in teams, where again the energy creates ambition, creates goals, creates and achieves and maintains your values and beliefs.

Hypnosis is another strategy which allows your mind to remove the present and go into its subconscious or unconscious thoughts. It can help you to put these thoughts in order, remove the things that are unimportant to you, which are holding back your ability to achieve and replace them with energy which is truly focused. Meditation is a form of self-hypnosis.

An interesting exercise is to create a dream board or a goal board. This works by thinking about something you really want to achieve. Try to vision it, try to see what it would look like and then build a large board with cuttings and ideas of what this goal or dream will look like. For instance if one of your dreams is to have a country house on a lake with lots of birds, cut out pictures of what this would look like, paste them onto a board and put the board where you see it every day. This has a remarkable effect on the likelihood getting it! Your unconscious and subconscious mind continually directs that energy towards helping make your dream come true. When it becomes a conscious thought it usually happens.

You can use those thoughts to set SMART goals, which will be linked to positive and compelling visions. With goals, the better the clarity, the more likely the achievement.

Synchronicity

I am sure that you have gone to the telephone to make a phone call and you pick it up to dial the number and the person you were gong to call is calling you at the same time. If you are on holiday and you think of somebody, they often appear. Also what happens is that you like a particular car and you are thinking about it when you are out and about. You have never seen one on the street before, and suddenly they appear. This is because our thoughts create energy and the reticular activator in our brain processes the thoughts, sends out energetic messages that bring extraordinary results often known as synchronicity.

For me an example of synchronicity was when I had to travel on business to South Africa. My cousin who lives there said *"How about you come over tonight for dinner?"* I said I was *"far too tired"* but she insisted. She said she would pick me up, which she did. When I walked into her home and into the sitting room, I saw someone I didn't immediately recognise. Then I realised that it was my own brother who had been thrown out, because of his long hair, from Zimbabwe. He had been travelling for eighteen months and he arrived there exactly the same day as I did. A remarkable thing, it was also my father's birthday.

An encounter with Patch Adams

Some experiences just need to be recorded. Meeting Patch Adams in Macclesfield is one of those experiences. Maybe you've seen the film, starring Robin Williams, that dramatises his life? Well, in person, he was every bit as impressive as I had hoped and maybe just a little more. Patch, in person, is an inspiration. He is both a medical doctor and a clown and he uses both skills to help patients and to campaign for a better healthcare system in the USA. He believes that laughter, joy and creativity are an integral part of the healing process and therefore true health care must incorporate those elements.

So what should be the message that relates to Leaders from that? That they should also be clowns? Not exactly, but if laughter, joy and creativity can help to heal people, they can also prevent illness in the first place. So much illness in the workplace comes from stress and from a lack of motivation and it is preventable. So, leaders may not need to become clowns, but they should be caring for their employees and giving them space in which they can have fun whilst still performing well for the company.

If **laughter** *is the* **best medicine,**
maybe it can **also** *be the*
best motivator

Keeping fit to lead

There is no need to be an Olympic athlete, but you do need to be able to function. Mental conditioning is supported by physical conditioning and we need to take some form of physical exercise in order to lead a team – especially the complex of teams that is a growing business.

Keeping yourself is as important as keeping the business in a good state of health. A good way of doing this is modelling the behaviour that you want yourself. If you set a model example of fitness, diet and rejuvenation, you will get that within your organisation. You will get a fitter organisation. Your people will consider their health and their wellness and in that way the people and their business will continue to thrive.

Despite our best efforts, we all get ill sometimes. It is a fact of life and one that, for most of us, may mean a day or two on reduced power or off work altogether. Sometimes, though, illness is longer lasting and may disrupt a business significantly. It may affect the leader, too. There are two aspects that the business and the Leader need to consider – the person and the role.

The best place for long term health concerns is out in the open. Don't avoid the conversation because the person who is facing those concerns most likely wants to talk to you about them. Their concerns about themselves and their family will be mirrored by their concerns about their job and about the role they should be playing for you. By sharing the concerns, you open a conversation that will allow you to understand the circumstances and to make plans to deal with them in the best way for both the business and the employee.

When the person who has long term health problems is also the Chief Executive, then it is important that he or she discusses them with their closest colleagues, the Board, non-executives and the Chairman or with the management team, so that plans can be made to cover the role as needed. Most Chief Executives carry some of their plans and knowledge in their head. If the illness is severe, there is likely to be a period of uncertainty following the onset and in that period, the business is vulnerable.

Policies and planning are crucial here, if you want to manage the business through illness smoothly and without loss of momentum. Work with what you know – that all of us are vulnerable to illness and accident – and formulate a strategy, at least for the key people in the organisation, that will ensure that someone can cover the role at short notice. When we consider other risks to the business, such as competition, product failures, manufacturing downtime and the like, we also need to consider our people. A clear policy on sickness and absence will make it easy for your team to understand what happens to them, in work terms, when they are ill, and remove uncertainty.

Company private health insurance can reduce the amount of time your key people are left waiting for important medical procedures and permanent health policies can ensure that employees are covered when sick pay runs out.

Finally, formal work shadowing can ensure that someone is always there who can pick up a role quickly and prevent unintended consequences from occurring. People continuity is part of business continuity – a very important part.

So, look after yourself, but ensure that if the worse should happen, you're covered.

Let me ask you a question. At the weekend do you work on business issues, write a paper, speak to colleagues about the business – or did you take two *(or more)* days off work?

Did you listen to the news first thing in the morning? When you think about it, when there is so much bad news, is this a good way to start your day in a positive frame of mind?

In a period where full time working hours are falling, it is my – entirely unscientific – experience that leaders, especially those in charge of small and growing businesses, will have been working over holiday periods. So many more business people work some or all of their time from home and most can now access their emails and files whilst at home. As business continues to become a competitive, 24-hour world for more businesses, is it that surprising that more will succumb to the temptation of 'just finishing that report' or 'catching up with my emails'.

I'm not saying that doing some work during holidays and weekends is a bad thing. Quite the opposite. For some people it is the only time they get where they can leave behind the clamour of daily business life and think. Some of their most creative work happens in the relative peace of the weekend. What I am saying, though, is that too much work in the time that could be used for recreation can become a problem. The clue is in the word 're-creation'. Even when the pressure is on at its most demanding, we all need time away from those pressures to rebuild. Far from being a waste of time, time spent in recreation can recharge your batteries so that you are much more productive when you resume work. By taking regular breaks and doing something with family or friends, your overall productivity will increase.

It may be tempting to believe that, by working harder we can finally break through to a better place. The truth is that working smarter will allow you to get to a better place more quickly.

Reversing the Ageing Process

In an earlier chapter, I commented on how I hear friends, some of them considerably younger than myself, say, 'I can't remember things', 'I can't remember names', 'I can't do this', 'I can't walk any further', 'I can't do my job' and the excuse is always that 'I'm getting older'. I have an unlimited belief that I can do anything that I want to do and, as I get older, I can do it better, with more wisdom and more experience. I want to examine the idea that keeping fit is about both body and mind and how important it is to remain active mentally.

We hear a lot about the role that retired people and older people can play in business and, sometimes, opinion can be a little negative about the skills and performance of older people. This is a point of view with which I strongly disagree. Some older people just get better with age. I'm now 73 years old and past the 'retirement' age that is the norm and I feel that I'm giving better advice and doing better consultancy work than I've ever done.

The secret is, I believe, that of keeping your mind active. Medical science is extending our life expectancy with better treatments and drugs but we can waste all that extra life if we let our minds get flabby. So, whether you choose crosswords and sudoku or business or charitable work, you need to keep stretching your mind. The brain is a muscle that needs exercising just the same as all of our other muscles.

Ever wondered how old you really are? Not the number of years since your birth but rather the attitudes and habits that you adopt can determine your real age. There have been television programmes about reducing the age you appear to be and there is a website www.realage.com that offers a test you can do to determine your real age. You can then browse pages of advice on how to reduce that real age.

Once, retirement was considered to be 'the scrapheap' after which you just waited patiently for the end, which often came quite quickly. It is no longer like that. Older people have huge stores of life experience and knowledge that they can offer to business and business should be using it. It takes some adjustments on both sides. Older people need to communicate with business in a way that means they will be listened to and business people, especially the younger element, need to put aside prejudices about older people and approach them with an open mind. Businesses will gain depth and consideration in their decision-making and older people will have the opportunity to continue living a much more valuable life.

Age *is* **no longer** *a* **barrier,** *unless you choose to make it so*

A word of advice to my 'older' readers. You will find that many older people do not achieve because they believe that their minds weaken as they get older. This is sometimes influenced by what they read in the media or they expect to have some form of dementia. I am sure that if you believe that, then it is definitely true for you! You can take action and change that belief, and you will find that you can carry on achieving at whatever age you are. I know I have. I seem to be an inspiration to many people in my business and social network. I know that they are impressed by someone my age that keeps doing more, not less, as the years go by. For me, it is simple. I just focus on what I want to do and do not let age be a limiting factor.

I learned to ski when I was 65. Before I went skiing the first time, I was assaulted by 'good advice' given to me by friends and family. They said things like 'you're getting older, do you really think this is a sensible thing to be doing at your age?' I think they really thought I had lost it!

I had doubts whether I could really do this as I had never done anything like this before. It's interesting because what drove me was the fact that I was with my own group – the leader of that group and therefore I couldn't fail. I had to demonstrate I was the leader even though I wasn't as good as them; I had to try, as that is what I am always teaching them to do all the time. What was driving me was the need to demonstrate leadership and that is something which is really good learning for everybody.

Standing on top of a mountain for the first time was really scary almost frozen like the snow. I didn't want to move. I was with one of my group who was actually more scared than I was – he was scared of the height whilst I was scared of falling over. As soon as I pushed myself by saying *'you have got to be the leader here Brian'* the exhilaration/movement was just fantastic. The fact that my colleague then started to follow me – going down the hill was still scary but also a wonderful feeling of what leadership is all about.

Starting a business at the age of 59 was also not something a lot of people would do. They might think it is time to wind down, time to start doing less. I found I couldn't subscribe to that kind of thinking. And more important, I had to make sure that I didn't take their beliefs on board!

This belief is so powerful that I subsequently started three other companies and I am on the board of three other companies as Chairman and am considering, at the age of 73, starting another new business as I am confident of being able to lead this one as well.

The alternative for me was a slow death. My belief is that, at the age of 73, we still have most of the brain which we had when we were 25. My brain is still active and I don't forget things, but what I have done, and still do, is to treat the brain as a muscle that has to be used. The more it is used, the stronger I will be, the longer I will live and the more wisdom I will be able to deliver. So not doing it means that the brain will die, the muscle won't get used and then I will slowly die – therefore it was not a choice for me NOT to do it!

Keep your mind active, learn more things and keep making the offer to do things in your business, with your family and your friends. Put out the energy and things will come to you.

Never *be* **satisfied** *with the status quo*

You must also recognise that life is for living and not for wasting. Consider doing new things – meet new people and ensure that you don't miss out. One way to ensure that you achieve is to believe and to understand that givers really do gain[20] . Every time you give, you get more back in spades.

I can't complete this dialogue without sharing with those of you who have had the patience to read to the end of the book, the learning that I have received through my network of friends that have given me the wisdom to develop myself and therefore able to model the delivering this wisdom to the benefit of all the people that I know and work with who then pass on these valuable lessons.

Sue Knight and NLP

The story starts with meeting Sue Knight who, approximately 18 years ago, was a member of my TEC group and who I therefore spent time working with to help develop her own life. Subsequently, as I got to know Sue better, she became my coach and mentor and still is to this day. Sue became prominent through her experience of NLP – Neuro Linguistic Programming - and her books on the subject. She used her method of teaching the use of NLP with me on a continuing basis. I embraced this learning which gave me a number of tools to be able to inspire others to develop themselves in mind, body and soul. So much so that, when I started the Academy for Chief Executives some 14 years ago, I embodied this learning into the organisation and inspired many of our chairmen and members to work with Sue by developing our own courses and using her within our organisation and our members' businesses. Much of the uniqueness and the success of the Academy has been the development of the soft skills and Sue had been prominent in this. I acknowledge that the coaching mentoring, teaching and inspiration from my friend and teacher Sue Knight has been important to the success of the Academy.

In January 2007, Sue Knight ran a two week NLP intensive course in Kerala, Southern India. For the first time, my wife attended an NLP course with me. Every day on the beach we did yoga, my first experience of this. Our yoga master was Swami Radni Krishna Chatanya. The yoga took me by surprise in the value that it brought me and the interest that grew within me regarding the techniques.

[20]**The concept of 'givers gain' is widely attributed to Dr Ivan R Misner, founder of BNI and is the 'strap line' of that organisation. http://www.bni.com**

Sue brought Swami Ji into one of our meeting days as a model of excellence and it turns out he is a healer and a remarkable man. He took my pulse and from that reading was able to tell me that I had a heart issue, which I knew, but the surprising thing was he said it could be cured, whereas my cardiologist said it could only be kept stable.

Had I been writing this prior to that and asked 'when do I intend to retire' I would have said as a metaphor – at age 123. Where that came from I do not know. Later, towards the end of this course where the whole group were saying I should take the advice offered by Swami Ji, he invited us to meet his teacher, Yogi Swami Bua Ji, who was moving his business from New York to Kerala. We had a special opportunity to meet him with thousands of his disciples. It was a very important meeting for me, as this yogi, senior swami, is in the Guinness book of Records for being able to blow a conch for 5¼ hours without taking a breath and breathing through his eyes. It turns out he is 123, probably now 124, speaks 13 languages, still does yoga every morning and walks. A remarkable man and he was quite prepared to debate any of the thoughts we had and to deliver his own wisdom.

I came back to the UK and started to read about ayurvedic medicine and the health qualities that were available and their beliefs around not taking pills. I met three other people who inspired me on to the next stage. They were Sue's NLP and Indian partner Ashok Subramanian, my Indian partner Rakash Bhargava and Nandita Shah a medical doctor from Delhi.

After about three or four months, Swami Ji said he was prepared to give me the medicines to see if they would cure me, which in fact was under control by taking statins and blood pressure pills. He said he would not give the medicines until I became a vegan. This set me back a long way, as it was a huge step for me to take. Although I had been a vegetarian for the last year and ate fish, being a vegan was a step too far. I thought further and talked to Rakesh and Ashok, both of whom are vegans and realised there could be some real value in changing my lifestyle by becoming a vegan. This would be helpful not only in the control of my heart problem but also in the development of my body and soul to meet my goal of living to 123, so I used my normal method of dealing with major change and decided to become a vegan for 21 days.

The change in my body was dramatic. I immediately started to lose weight, my cholesterol improved; my blood pressure didn't change much but as my weight came down this clearly improved my mobility. I felt I was becoming brighter and was able to develop wisdom at a level higher than prior to my becoming a vegan.

NLP in Kerala

The story moves to a year later when again I attended, with Jacky, Sue Knight's NLP course in Kerala. I saw Swami Ji who said things had improved and it was reversing the aging process, however it was very slow and there was a lot more room for improvement. He recommended I took 15 herbal medicines that I had already tried once. It was very difficult and after a week of the course he recommended that I spend 24 days at the Institute for Naturology and Yoga Sciences in Bangalore *(now the Jindal Naturecure Institute[21]).* The following August I made the decision that I was going to do this and as a result, I am dictating this on the last day of my 24 days. The JNI is a business run as a charity started by Mr Jindal and is a cross between a hospital, a health spa and a prison. There is no drinking, no smoking, no using laptops, limited use of mobile phones and many, many other strict rules designed to help you to stick to the diet that is devised for you. You are under a doctor and the yoga doctor and on the premises is a complete hospital with ECG, CAT scans etc. People that have issues around weight, heart disease, diabetes, allergies, back pains etc could really benefit from this approach and certainly my body is leaner, meaner and fitter for this stay. The benefits go far beyond that of the body, the cleansing of the mind and soul are very apparent and I am leaving in a position of really believing that I can demonstrate that I have extended my life, enhanced my business acumen and am ready to inspire leaders to achieve their dreams and that my dream will come true.

The particular learning that comes from the study of naturopathy, which does contain certain aspects of ayurvedic thinking in that everything is natural. As Dr. Nandita Shah says in her session Peas v Pills[22] , the whole of our health can be managed really quite simply and at JNI we learnt the value of water. We are what we eat and therefore careful diet is important along with walking and above all the value of yoga. There seems to be a cure, an asana, a yogic method of dealing with all sorts of health issues. At JNI there were some ten yoga teachers and during the private lessons with me the yoga master created a set of asanas that particularly were suited to my issues of high blood pressure and minor heart disease. So the inspiration is that by walking, drinking water and doing yoga and eating carefully

---

[21]**http://www.jindalnaturecure.org/**
[22]**http://www.leap-auroville.com/course-topics/healing-health/peas-vs-pills-dr-nandita-shah/**

as a vegetarian, you can increase your energy, your wisdom, brain power and stay fit in mind, body and soul.

It is my belief that I can do anything and anyone can do anything that involves changing a habit given that they do it for 21 days. I have proved this to myself by first becoming a vegetarian and then a vegan. Now over the last 21 days at the Jindal Naturecure Institute through very strict diet and control, drinking lots of water and a yogic methodology, I have again demonstrated how anyone can carry on delivering the wisdom and pleasure that they wish too. **Certainly to an age well over 100!!**

Above: *Swami Radni Krishna Chatanya - the Monk that changed my life.*

Timeline

YEAR	SIGNIFICANT EVENT	EFFECTIVE LEARNING
1936	Born, started to learn- crying, eating, walking , talking and laughing.	You have to get up when you fall down.
1941	Allowed at the age of four and a half to travel to school by bus on my own.	To have the confidence to make my own decisions and to be able to look after myself and to have responsibility for myself.
1946 ish	Father installed two lessons that I have followed all my life. The 1st never to start eating until everyone has been served.	To respect your host and your parents and therefore the unwritten rules and laws of society.
1946 ish	The 2nd to always walk on the outside if walking with a woman.	Manners are important and give respect to women.
1951 ish	Friends and family insisted that it was bad to volunteer.	I believed them and never did until later in life when it always put me in a good position and I have now ended up being proactive rather than reactive.
1951 14.5	Left school at 14+ with a chip on my shoulder having not passed any exams. Forced to study classes I had no empathy for while subjects I had an interest in were restricted to me.	Told continually I underachieved resulting in low self esteem.
1951	Compensated by attending night school without any great success.	My style of learning was not academic but experiential and therefore continued to fail.
1951	1st employment at an accountants, loved it although it cost me more to get to and from work than I earned. Needed to work as a gardener to make ends meet. Lived in London away from home.	Again learned to be self sufficient and responsible for my own development.

YEAR	SIGNIFICANT EVENT	EFFECTIVE LEARNING
1952 15.5	2nd job local council; Wages Clerk at the Borough Treasurers in my home town in Margate. Responsible for paying salaries to hundreds of workers throughout town.	*Learned that I was able to take major responsibility.*
1953 16.5	Lost job that I loved due to person returning from National Service and it was 'last in first out'.	*Devastated and another blow to my self esteem.*
1953 17.5	3rd job working as a bank counter clerk with lots of responsibility, told I did a great job but needed bank exams to get on. Not possible as I needed basic O levels first and National Service was looming.	*That my failure to achieve at school was to really hold me back and caused me to look for alternative ways to learn.*
1953 17.5	I volunteered to sign on in the RAF for 3 years. I believed that I was wasting my time at the bank and if I signed up six months early and stayed for another six months I would get the benefit of being full time. This was a decision I took and implemented on my own	*My self esteem went up as I passed all the tests and was accepted my parents were proud of me when I told them after the event.*
1954	Huge shock to go through the RAF discipline and structure but went with it and volunteered for everything I could.	*Self esteem kept rising as I passed exams and was given more responsibility.*
1954	Lost I.D. card serious military offence, punishment followed and virtually put in prison for 7 days.	*Learnt about team work and team support as the whole billet supported me and helped me through the perceived disgrace.* *Gave birth to my belief that all people are equal.*

YEAR	SIGNIFICANT EVENT	EFFECTIVE LEARNING
1955	Volunteered to go abroad and was accepted to go to Gibraltar for two years.	*Proved to myself that volunteering was good. Was given massive responsibility in managing people and loved it and was appreciated and received more promotion. Self esteem really high.*
1957 21	Left RAF returned home to parents who now lived in London. Joined Uncle's East End linen business.	
1957	Although my Uncle was a very religious man, an incident involving the honesty of one of his managers and the lack of support from my uncle forced me to leave.	*I realised that I could not work in a company that compromised my principles. Maybe my principles are different to others but they are very important to me.*
1957	Joined the John Lewis Partnership as a Junior on the circuit in Peter Jones, Sloane Square, London.	*Delighted to have been accepted without formal qualifications and delighted be back in a structured business. I volunteered for everything and joined in the whole culture of the business.*
1958	Started studying for the National Retail Distribution Certificate.	*First exam to pass with distinction and requested to start teaching the subject. Esteem at an all time high.*
1959 23	Met and fell in love with Jaclyn who has been my wife now for 48 years.	*That with give and take a marriage can be sustainable and happy over all these years.*
1960	Managing Director, Lionel Wharrad, took notice of my progress and promoted me twice.	*Loved the responsibility and thrived under the partnership culture of the John Lewis Partnership.*

YEAR	SIGNIFICANT EVENT	EFFECTIVE LEARNING
1960	Left John Lewis, travelled to Canada and worked at House of Ideas for 6 months.	*Expanded my knowledge and still looking for greener grass.*
1961 25	Rejoined John Lewis further promotions followed. Returned to marry Jaclyn.	*Kept getting promotion and became a star of the Managing Director, Lionel Wharrad.*
1964	Bombshell, Lionel Wharrad told me I could go no further as I had no degree and I needed one to go further. First daughter Judy was born.	*Massive blow and damaging to my self esteem.*
1965 29	Lionel leaves to join Bookers, I was headhunted by him to open a new department store as buyer.	*Self esteem returned as this was a wonderful opportunity.* *Learnt how to be a board member and to understand strategy.*
	Promoted head buyer, 4 more stores followed.	*Self esteem running high and loved being in such and interesting and important position.*
	Duties now included buying for the overseas stores as well.	*This continued and, being with Lionel, we had the same culture around people as we had at John Lewis.*
1966 30	A period in Trinidad and Guyana as a department store consultant followed and at the age of 30 I was making suggestions to the Managing Directors of these well established department stores.	*My first experience as a consultant while still running buying department.*
1967	Bookers purchase a chain of retail shops selling linens and curtains. Involved in the buying and brand development. Second daugher Rachel was born.	*We totally re-branded them and I learnt a lot about branding and marketing.*
1968	My brother was killed in a car crash.	

YEAR	SIGNIFICANT EVENT	EFFECTIVE LEARNING
1970 *34*	Big blow. Bookers decide to go to food only.	*Jobs are not for life.*
	Promoted to joint MD responsible for selling the retail group.	*Realised how little understanding I had of the accounts function as thought we were doing brilliantly.*
1970	Sold stores, new positions offered by Bookers but I decided to go with the group that purchased Herald shops. Third daugher Anna was born.	
	Became trouble shooter and PA to the group Managing Director but left after a year as I hated the values that he ran the business on.	*I learned how the values I had learnt over the last ten years were so important to a happy and successful organisation.*
1973 *37*	Joined H Goldman as a main Board Director to help them professionalise and to float the company on the London stock exchange.	*Major learning how to change the whole culture of a family run company still controlled by its founder to a professional public company that has responsibilities to its shareholders.* *Learned a lot about computers as I had the initial responsibility for a major computer installation.*
	Became MD of the cash and carry business in Hackney. Expanded the business by a further 9 warehouses.	*Built on my learning about running a wholesale business on low margins and all the issues relating to warehousing, stock loss, managing people on the lower end of the salary scale.*

YEAR	SIGNIFICANT EVENT	EFFECTIVE LEARNING
1977 *41*	Parent Company takes on new Chairman, Roy Garner . He advises major changes to stay solvent and encourages me to sell the Cash and Carry group to raise money for the core business and then recommends that I do a management buyout of the last two depots. This I successfully do with the help of venture capital that I raise myself.	*Learned how to negotiate the sale and then to raise capital to start my own organisation.*
	Initial founder of Landmark, that became the largest independent buying group in the UK.	*Learned the politics of dealing with the board of a voluntary buying group.*
	Sold the second unit then concentrated on building the remaining C & C warehouse.	
	Acquired adjacent building when BRS were denationalised. Extended the sales area to over 100,000 square feet.	
	Became Chairman of Landmark.	
	Acquired Esposito catering business	
	Major financial problem but traded through it and was well on road to full recovery when financial backer pulled support.	*Learned yet again not to trust figures that were presented but to fully understand them myself.*
1981 *46*	Sold bushiness through receivership.	*Some of the most important learning in that I learned how to deal with this huge emotional blow to my self esteem.* *I learned how people can let you down despite giving them shares and I also learned who will stand by you through good and bad.*

YEAR	SIGNIFICANT EVENT	EFFECTIVE LEARNING
1982 *47*	Opened Tredegar Cash and Carry Ltd. My father died.	*Learned how to win back suppliers and to develop a new brand. Learned how to overcome the emotional blow and restructure a new organisation regaining trust self esteem.*
1983 *48*	Started a video company at the outset of the video business. Expanded to 5 video wholesale leasing units. Called this Tredegars Home Entertainment.	*Learned to back my judgement and start a new business within the Cash and Carry which became the leader in its field of renting video films to the small retailer who then rented it on to the consumer.*
1986 *50*	Sold Tredegars Home Entertainment to major PLC Hillsdown Holdings and sold the successful Cash and Carry to concentrate on the video business. With Hillsdown, we increased the concession departments nationally to 40 separate concessions around the UK and Ireland.	*Learned how to deal with the politics of a conglomerate PLC where they supported us while organisation was doing well and were unhelpful when not.*
1987	My mother died	
1988 *51*	Bought the rights to an invention that would vend video films.	*Learned the difficulties in dealing with inventors and getting the invention working. Invested £1,000,000 to get a working model. Considerable interest in the invention but sold very few due to production challenges.*

YEAR	SIGNIFICANT EVENT	EFFECTIVE LEARNING
1990 *53*	Hillsdown received an offer from Canada for £3,000,000 which offered me a great opportunity and it was accepted. Night before completion the purchasing company failed to deliver the funds. Hillsdown decided to accept an offer of £300,000 for the business and out voted me. I was not sold with the business.	*Learned how to deal with the disappointment and having to leave the team and find new employment.*
1990 *53*	Became an independent consultant management consultant working with a firm of accountants. Applied and obtained a contract with the Department of Trade and Industry helping businesses get and manage a match funded grant for consultancy called the Enterprise Initiative. Available for Business Planning, Quality or Manufacturing.	*During this period saw 100 companies and assessed them for the various grants and then followed it up by checking the outcomes. Massive learning about all sizes of companies and recognized that my knowledge was extensive.*
1990	Came to the realisation that I could do the main consultancy for Business Planning and did two sweetheart consultancies and submitted them to the DTI and received their approval to be a registered consultant to take on this work. During the next two years completed some 12 consultancies in different sectors, with great success.	*Great learning in creating rapport with staff and analysis of the situation and preparing long reports, then selling the ideas to the board.*
1991 *54*	Became an Investor in People consultant and passed the test to become an inspector.	*Learned the new government initiative that gave businesses a plaque for being a good employer.*

YEAR	SIGNIFICANT EVENT	EFFECTIVE LEARNING
1991	I now had a thriving practice working with government funding and on my own. Writing long reports was not where I wanted to be, I preferred to be at the sharp end working with teams and being involved with the implementation and the creative side of businesses.	*Learned what my strengths were and what I liked and hated to do.*
1992 55	In late 1991 I was offered a position to take over running a group for The Executive Committee an organisation started in America in 1957 and started in the UK in 1988 by a licensee of the American organisation. I accepted the opportunity and after intensive interviews was accepted to takeover the group that was being run by the company Managing Director.	*Learned that these were groups totally focused on learning and learning experientially through peer group meetings and one to one coaching. This seemed to play to all my strengths. I was dropped in the deep and without any training and thrived. This was followed by intensive training in America.*
1992 to 1996	I loved the work and gradually gave up all my other interests to run several groups of CEOs and two groups of Directors called Key Groups.	*I learnt how to be a great executive coach and to inspire the group members to stay within the group for an average of 4 years.*
	During this time I had a member, Sue Knight, who was developing a set of tools called Neuro Linguistic Programming. At the time I was coaching Sue. However she soon turned the tables and got me interested in NLP and how I could use it to inspire the Managing Directors in my groups.	*I studied NLP with Sue and rate it as the most important piece of learning and now use it as my basic tools for inspiring leaders and continuing to develop myself.*

YEAR	SIGNIFICANT EVENT	EFFECTIVE LEARNING
1996 *59*	In early 1996 I was approached by the franchise owner and asked if I would take over from the current Managing Director. I readily agreed and it really excited me. I gave up two of my groups ready to takeover in July 1996. Three months before I was told that although I was in lead position the franchise owner wanted six months more to make a decision. I found this decision unacceptable and after further discussion decided to leave.	*The learning was how unpredictable people are and with all there wisdom could not be transparent and were able to be unreasonable.*
1996 to 2008 *71*	All the groups that I was running - 33 members - said, after intensive meeting and discussion with the franchise owner, that they thought he was unreasonable and if I started on my own they would join me. I did a deal with TEC and agreed not to recruit new members for 6 months and THE ACADEMY FOR CHIEF EXECUTIVES Limited was born.	*STILL run a group myself and now have 40 groups, one in Manhattan and about to start in India. My learning is that my entire career was developed to do this work. I am never bored, rarely write reports and continually inspire other to achieve their dreams.* *My plan is to carry on doing this until my health stops me and this can be when I am over 100.*
2009 *72*	Late in 2009, I decided that it was really important for me to have a succession plan and to consider selling the business. However, I wanted to do it on the basis that I still had involvement for the rest of my life, as the plan is for me to carry on delivering wisdom for the rest of my life.	*Ongoing discussions to reach a succession plan that works for me, my chairmen and all of our members.*

YEAR	SIGNIFICANT EVENT	EFFECTIVE LEARNING
2009 72	There have been many offers to buy the business during these 13 years and I have walked away from most of them as either they were offering insufficient money for the value of the business or the likelihood is that they would destroy the business and merge it with their own business . They certainly would not carry on with the culture that I created and, as I wish to stay part of that business, it was not appropriate. Great learning all the time about the reason why people wish to purchase companies.	*Middle of 2008 the country ran into a major recession due to complete failure of the banks and complete lack of integrity at the highest level. It was therefore necessary for us to survive and for us to ensure that our members survived.* *The learning that I have had over the years on how to survive came in really valuable and I came up with 14 ways to survive and something which we have had to take on board ourselves as well.*

This summary of my business life will give some background
to how the stories, anecdotes and beliefs in this book have
come about.

Brian Chernett - 2010

Lightning Source UK Ltd.
Milton Keynes UK
UKOW04f1649030913

216481UK00001B/6/P